DEVELOPING DISCIPLES OF CHRIST

Understanding the Critical Relationship
between Catechesis and Evangelization

JULIANNE STANZ

THE EFFECTIVE CATECHETICAL LEADER

Series Editor Joe Paprocki, DMin

LOYOLAPRESS.
A JESUIT MINISTRY
Chicago

LOYOLA PRESS.
A JESUIT MINISTRY

3441 N. Ashland Avenue
Chicago, Illinois 60657
(800) 621-1008
www.loyolapress.com

Cover art credit: maglyvi/iStock/Thinkstock.

ISBN: 978-0-8294-4528-2
Library of Congress Control Number: 2017948832

Printed in the United States of America.
17 18 19 20 21 22 23 24 25 26 27 Versa 10 9 8 7 6 5 4 3 2 1

Contents

Welcome to The Effective Catechetical Leader Series

The **Effective Catechetical Leader** series provides skills, strategies, and approaches to ensure success for leaders of parish faith-formation programs. It will benefit anyone working with catechists, including Directors of Religious Education, pastors, diocesan directors, and catechetical training programs. Combining theory and practice, this series will

- provide practical instruction and printable resources;
- define the role of the catechetical leader and offer specific and practical strategies for leading, collaborating, and delegating;
- offer approaches for leading and catechizing in a more evangelizing way; and
- describe best practices for recruiting, training, and forming catechists; developing a vision for faith formation; forming an advisory board; planning and calendaring; networking with colleagues; selecting quality catechetical resources; handling the administrative aspects of the ministry; and identifying various groups to be catechized and approaches that meet the unique needs of those various groups.

Whether you are starting out as a catechetical leader or have been serving as one for many years, **The Effective Catechetical Leader** series will help you use every aspect of this ministry to proclaim the gospel and invite people to discipleship.

About This Book

St. Pope John Paul II reminds us in *Catechesi Tradendae* that catechesis is a moment—"a very remarkable one—in the whole process of evangelization." In other words, catechesis is an essential part of evangelization, not something separate from it. Therefore, it is critically important that catechetical leaders recognize how to effectively catechize in a way that advances the Church's primary mission to evangelize. To that end, this third volume of **The Effective Catechetical Leader** will explore a Catholic understanding of evangelization grounded in Scripture and Tradition, how the New Evangelization supports and enhances today's catechesis, the inseparable nature of content and methodology in catechesis, the absolute importance of adult catechesis, and so much more.

Teachable moments

1

What, on Earth, Are We Doing?
The Church Exists to Evangelize

Why Do We Fear the Word *Evangelization?*

What do you think of when you hear the word *evangelization?* Does it call to mind images of well-known televangelists such as Billy Graham, T. D. Jakes, Joyce Meyer, or Joel Osteen? Does it conjure up the sound of a knock on the door from someone who asks if you have accepted Jesus as your personal Lord and Savior? Maybe it has become synonymous with sending money overseas to children in developing countries. If you have thought any of these things about evangelization, you are certainly not alone.

The word *evangelize* comes from the Greek word meaning "to bring the Good News." Seems simple enough, right? And yet it seems that many Catholics are afraid of the word *evangelization* and barely use it at all. "Isn't there a better word than *evangelization?*" I have often been asked. "Something not so scary or intimidating, perhaps?" "Maybe we can call it something else?" The word *it* holds the key to why many Catholics find it difficult to share their faith with others: part of the difficulty lies in thinking about faith in "it" terms rather than in "who" terms.

Many of us have received a knock on the door from people belonging to other denominations, hoping to talk to us about their faith. A friend of mine named Michael told me that when he hears that people are going door-to-door in his neighborhood, he turns off all the lights in his house and locks the door! When the doorbell rings, he ignores it and then peeks out his window a few minutes later to make sure nobody is there. When I asked him why he doesn't want to engage with Jehovah's Witnesses, he gave me three reasons:

1. He doesn't want to be bothered on a busy evening when he would rather be doing something else.
2. He finds going door to door in such a manner to be aggressive and annoying.
3. He doesn't know his Catholic faith well enough and doesn't feel comfortable talking about it.

Number three was the biggest reason for Michael. He felt he didn't have the right words and wouldn't know how to respond or defend his faith. This is true for many people. But our faith is so much more than knowing all the answers or being able to cite Scripture verses when prompted!

At the heart of evangelization is nurturing a personal relationship with Christ, who is the same "yesterday and today and for ever" (Heb. 13:8). If my friend could share his heartfelt understanding of why his faith is important to him, who knows what surprises a knock on the door might hold for him?

The Deepest Identity of the Church

Pope Paul VI makes it very clear in his encyclical *Evangelii Nuntiandi* that the Church "exists in order to evangelize" (EN no.14). Evangelization is the "deepest identity" of the Church. The mandate to evangelize comes from Jesus Christ himself! Jesus commanded us, "Go therefore and make disciples of all nations, baptizing them in the name of the Father and of the Son and of the Holy Spirit, and teaching them to obey everything that I have commanded you" (Matt. 28:19–20). Jesus is the center of evangelization and the heart of catechesis. We share not just the message of Christ but his very person. Jesus *is* the Good News. In your role as a catechetical leader, you are called to ensure that catechesis and evangelization are seen by all as inseparable partners.

Why did Christ want us to share him and his message with the world? Jesus' mission was to bring all to his Father, God the Father who is our Father. It is Jesus who accomplishes his Father's work, the salvation of all by his redemptive suffering, Death, and Resurrection. It is in and through Jesus that the fullness of God's eternal plan is unfolded in our catechetical efforts. Jesus is "the message, the messenger, the purpose of the message, and the consummation of the message" (*National Directory for Catechesis*, [Washington, DC: USCCB, 2005], 4). The commission to baptize using the formula of Father, Son, and Holy Spirit incorporates all Christians into Trinitarian love. This love is the fountain of love for everyone who chooses to accept it.

So why *are* Catholics so afraid of evangelization? Let's take a look at some of the reasons.

Evangelization: It Is a Catholic Thing!

Historically there are important reasons why Catholics are hesitant to see themselves as evangelizers, and it is important to be aware of them. I outline some reasons why Catholics have a fear of evangelization on the *Catechist's Journey* blog at www.catechistsjourney.loyolapress.com. As a catechetical leader, you will encounter the following attitudes in those you minister to.

The Immigrant Church

After giving a talk, I was approached by Anna, who enquired if evangelization was really a "Catholic thing" and wondered if it was an approved practice in the Catholic Church! She was under the impression that evangelization was the work of Protestants, and so this call to evangelize as Catholics was personally very difficult for her. After listening for some time, I realized that Anna's fear of evangelization was rooted in her parents' identity as Polish immigrants who had been oppressed for their faith. Many of Anna's childhood memories centered around "fitting in" to ensure that members of her family were considered good American citizens. Her parents did not speak of their faith openly and encouraged their children to keep silent when faith was discussed in public.

American Catholicism still carries within it a lingering historical memory of Catholics being set apart and viewed with suspicion because of their beliefs. In the late nineteenth and early twentieth centuries, urban-dwelling Catholics lived together in small, tight-knit communities where faith was at the root of their lives—the Irish on the South Side of Chicago, for example, or the Polish communities in Brooklyn, New York. During this time, horror stories circulated about how Catholic immigrants were treated. The message was clear: Catholicism should not be seen or heard in public. This desire to fit in had stayed with Anna throughout her life. Faith, she believed, was private and not meant to be discussed in public.

I remember the first morning I woke up in America after leaving Ireland in 2001 at the age of twenty-three. I could hear a coffeepot brewing rather than the familiar whistle of the teakettle that I grew up with. It was a reminder that I was no longer at home but somewhere new, different, and in many respects very foreign to me. Life became a series of culture shocks as I learned how to adjust to my new life in Wisconsin. While I was thankful that something familiar to me—our Catholic faith—does not change much from one country to the next, I also recognized that how people experienced their Catholic faith in this country has not been the same for all.

Faith as Private

The increasing unwillingness of immigrants to draw attention to themselves and their faith led to an erosion of the faith in the public square. Catholics bought into the lie that faith was to be kept private—and we have inherited the idea that this separation of "private" faith and public matters is appropriate. How many times, for example, have you heard Catholics say, "The Church should not comment on politics"? Many believe that the Church should offer no public commentary on the poor, on the misuse of resources, on systems that oppress others, on advancement, on science, and the list goes on and on. This belief, of course, goes against the core of the Gospel message! This dichotomy between faith and life was referenced by the Fathers of the Second Vatican Council in *Gaudium et Spes* when they wisely observed, "This split between the faith which many profess and their daily lives deserves to be counted among the more serious errors of our age" (43). But while faith is certainly personal, it is not meant to be a private matter.

A Post-Reformation Worldview

In the post-Reformation world, the Catholic response to Protestant Christianity was an increased focus on childhood catechesis. This stemmed from the belief that the Reformation could have been prevented if only young people had been reached sooner. Small Christian communities that had flourished since the early church became increasingly neglected. It was in these small Christian communities that faith had been shared and passed on from one generation to the next. This required that adults know the faith. When the focus shifted from adult catechesis to child-centered catechesis, the whole community lost.

Jesuit theologian Avery Dulles notes that in the centuries following the Protestant Reformation, Catholics have also avoided the term *evangelical* because of its general association with Protestant Christianity, especially the form of Christianity that stemmed from the great revivals of the eighteenth and nineteenth centuries. Catholics have tended not to focus historically on the intense, personal, biblical faith in Jesus Christ as Savior that characterizes many evangelical Christian denominations ("Evangelizing Theology," *First Things*, March 1996). Instead, Catholicism—particularly in the last five hundred years or so—has tended to focus on the organization, structure, and dogmatic formulations of the Church and on ensuring the validity of the sacraments. While it may seem paradoxical to refer to the Church as "evangelical," the very DNA of Catholicism *is* evangelization—a notion we will explore in the pages ahead.

Foreign Missions

In the past, evangelization focused on those who had never heard of Christ and his teachings. The mission field was seen as foreign, not domestic. "Sending money overseas to little pagan babies" was how one minister described missionary activity from the late 1950s to the early 1980s. Many Catholics born before the Second Vatican Council remember the plea for money to be sent overseas to the foreign missions. Throughout the last century, the work of evangelization and mission was increasingly seen as the purview of a select group of people—those who were called missionaries. This absolved many Catholics of the commission to make disciples. The imperative to evangelize was confined more and more to the professional class of people who worked for the Church rather than the average person in the pew.

Evangelization as Proselytizing

Many Catholics associate evangelization with proselytizing. "Oh, I don't want to push my religion on anyone else," people have often said

to me. Let's get this straight: Evangelization is not about proselytizing! It is about sharing the Good News of Jesus Christ—who he is and
what he has done for us—and inviting people to live out of that relationship. It is about witnessing to the saving love of a God who wants
his people to live in cooperation and joy with him. It is about a witness
so compelling and authentic that those who see it think, "What does
that person have?" and "Why does he or she live like that?" It is about
being able to give answers for our hope (1 Peter 3:15), reasons for our
beliefs, and witness to our story of faith!

Many Catholics are afraid of evangelizing because they do not want
to be accused of aggressive proselytizing. This is understandable. But
it might be helpful at this point to speak about what evangelization is
and what it is not in order to distinguish between the two—because
there are distinct differences between authentic evangelization and
over-zealous proselytizing.

What Evangelization Is and What It Is Not

The chart below outlines what evangelization is and what it is not.

	Evangelization Is:	Evangelization Is Not:
1.	Rooted in the person of Jesus Christ and his Body, the church.	Spreading an idea, philosophy, or ideology.
2.	Sharing your heartfelt understanding of how your life has been touched by God and your response to his love.	Having a neat and coherent response to every question that we may be asked.
3.	Living the joy of the Gospels each day so that others may wonder about the source of our joy.	Memorization of rote texts or Scripture verses so that we can pepper our conversations with them.

4.	Continually growing in an understanding of faith.	Dependent on our ability to regurgitate what we may have been taught in the tenth grade.
5.	Invitational, open, and dialogical.	Aggressive and seeking to condemn or ridicule.
6.	Dependent on the work of the Holy Spirit.	Dependent on our own work.
7.	Guiding people to see the light of Christ.	Imposing moral judgments.
8.	Encouraging people to look deeply and to seek beauty, truth, and goodness.	Slick marketing or promotional efforts.
9.	Understanding that the Lord already precedes us as we are made in his image and likeness. He has already saved us.	Making assumptions and being condescending toward others.

How do we, the Church, evangelize?

Evangelization aims at transforming hearts (interior change) and the world (external change). Too often, people think that door-to-door evangelization and standing on street corners are the only ways we can evangelize. But there are many ways that we, as Catholics, can evangelize. In *Evangelii Nuntiandi*, Pope Paul VI writes that evangelization includes

- catechesis
- preaching
- liturgy
- sacraments

- popular piety
- witness of the Christian life
- mass media
- personal contact

Me, an Evangelizer? You've Got to Be Kidding!

I was asked to give a talk to a gathering of catechetical leaders. Among this group were new catechetical leaders and those who had thirty-plus years of experience. I opened my talk by asking people to raise their hands if they were ministering in particular areas. Youth ministry? Several hands went up. RCIA? Another couple of hands went up. Then I asked if any were actively involved in the ministry of evangelization. Out of a room of two hundred ministers, only two raised their hands! Very few of those catechetical leaders identified with anything other than the ministry of catechesis. There was a stunned look when I reminded them that the term *catechesis* comes from the Greek word meaning "to echo" and that when they echoed the person of Christ and the teachings of the Church, they were evangelizing! "I never saw myself as being actively engaged in the ministry of evangelization," one person remarked.

Really!! ?

Each one of us is an evangelist first and a catechist second. So who is an evangelist? Repeat after me: "I am!"

The Characteristics of an Effective Evangelizer

You have entered catechetical leadership at a time in the Church when we have embarked on what is called the New Evangelization. In chapter 2 we will explore the New Evangelization in more depth. With that in mind, let's look at some essential attributes we need in order to be effective evangelizers.

1. **Love and knowledge.** An intellectual and affective appropriation of the faith is necessary to live a fully mature Catholic life. This is where the head meets the heart, where love of Christ and knowledge of Christ become integrated. In the words of Saint Catherine of Siena, "Love follows knowledge."

Head meets the ♡s

2. **Joy.** Pope Francis issued a call for all followers of Jesus to be a people filled with the joy of the risen Christ. Few people, if any, are attracted to a community whose members are finger-wagging, accusatory, or embittered.

3. **Boldness.** In proclaiming the gospel, the expression "He who dares, wins" is accurate. The early church was marked by disciples who were courageous and fearless. Conversations with those whom we love can often be difficult and distressing, but Christ says to each one of us, "Be of good cheer; I have overcome the world" (John 16:33, RSV). We must take risks to reach out to people if we expect to see a vibrant church filled with people from all different walks of life.

4. **Peace.** In the Mass we hear the words "Peace I leave with you; my peace I give to you" (John 14:27). It is clear that we need to reclaim a sense of peace in our world and in our lives. This is a peace that does not come from the world but comes only from faith in Christ.

In *Evangelii Gaudium*, Pope Francis also speaks of other "attitudes which foster openness to the message: approachability, readiness for dialogue, patience, a warmth and welcome which is non-judgmental" (165). As you examine this list of attributes, spend some time reflecting upon which attributes you have been gifted with and which attributes you need to strengthen.

It is important to remember that while we are all called to evangelize, the Holy Spirit is the actual agent of evangelization. We are the instruments called to evangelize and to be evangelized, but it is always the grace of the Holy Spirit that fuels the conversion.

But . . . Where Do I Start?

Saint Mother Teresa was once observed bathing the wounds of a person afflicted with leprosy. The smell was overpowering, and yet

Mother Teresa did not seem bothered at all. She took her time, gently and calmly washing the limbs of the suffering person. Afterward the observer said to her, "I wouldn't do that for a million dollars!" "Neither would I," she said, "but I would gladly do it for Christ."

This is at the heart of why we evangelize: to be the hands, voice, and feet of Christ to the one who is standing beside us. Evangelization *Amen, !* seeks to transform the world, one person at a time. Start with yourself, and then with those closest to you. Begin with your family, with your friends. Start with your catechists, and encourage your catechists to start with those closest to them—their family, friends, and students. *Recognize* Evangelization happens in one-on-one moments that are not planned *teachable* or scripted. We might not be comfortable thinking that evangelization *moments* happens outside of the parish, but it does and it should!

So, Where Does Catechesis Fit into All This?

If evangelization is the deepest identity of the church, you might be wondering, then how does catechesis fit in? Good question! The old adage that you shouldn't "put the cart before the horse" is one that we need to be mindful of when we speak of the relationship between evangelization and catechesis. Both evangelization and catechesis build upon each other and work together in the life of every person to bring him or her to a mature faith. One does not replace the other.

However, if attention is not given to the evangelization process, catechesis will not be as effective or fruitful. Correspondingly, if catechesis does not accompany evangelization, people will not be formed in the teachings and life of the Church and will struggle to understand what we say and do and why we believe what we believe. Catechesis is described in various Church documents as a "moment" or stage within the overall process of evangelization. We will explore this in more detail in chapter 5, but let's take a sneak preview here.

Catechesis Builds on Evangelization

Catechesis, which unfolds the beauty and treasures of Church teaching, presupposes that evangelization has already taken place. Catechesis is the "cart" behind the evangelization "horse." Evangelization aims to put people in touch with Jesus Christ, and catechesis builds upon this relationship and "formalizes" it. There is a reason that Pope Saint John Paul II called for a "new evangelization" and not a "new catechesis." We have more catechetical programs, materials, and resources than ever before in the history of the Church. While we must always strive to have strong, faithful, and dynamic catechesis, catechesis will not be fruitful in the life of a person unless he or she has been evangelized—that is, transformed by a relationship with Christ. It would be like handing someone a map or GPS without giving him a point of reference or telling her the destination. That person would wander all over the place blindly, without a sense of direction or purpose. Catechesis without evangelization just doesn't make any sense. We must introduce people to the "who" before we can share the "why."

Catechesis Is Formation for Life

Catechesis does not simply mean religious education. Education is a component of the catechetical enterprise, but catechesis arises out of evangelization. Catechesis is also not solely about the transmission of doctrine or information. While doctrinal formation is necessary, catechesis seeks the nourishment of the whole person so that he or she can live a well-formed, mature, and explicit life of faith.

Evangelize and Become Who You Are

We become an evangelizing church by becoming who we are intended to be as a church: the Body of Christ. This is an echo of the words of Saint Augustine, who reminded us that we should become what we see and receive who we are. All that we say and do should have as its source the Good News of the message and person of Jesus Christ, who wants to bring us all home to his Father through the power of the Holy Spirit. As catechetical leaders serving in this time of the New Evangelization, we have an indispensable role.

Now that we have looked at what evangelization is, let's examine what the New Evangelization is and what implications it holds for our ministry.

Summary: Your Last Will and Testament

"But you will receive power when the Holy Spirit has come upon you; and you will be my witnesses in Jerusalem, in all Judea and Samaria, and to the ends of the earth." (Acts 1:8)

In a sense, Jesus' last words are his last will and testament. He tells us, his disciples, that power will come to us when we receive the Holy Spirit so that we can be his witnesses to the ends of the earth. He leaves behind specific places where we should start: Jerusalem, Judea, and Samaria. Why these three places?

Jerusalem, as the most holy and sacred place, represents our home, or the center of the church's activities as the "domestic church." This is where we start: at home and in our parish. Next, Jesus names Judea. Judea was the neighborhood in which Jerusalem was located. So, after beginning at home, we are called to go out into our neighborhoods to spread the Good News. Last, Jesus asks us to go to Samaria. The Jews avoided Samaria and saw the Samaritans as outcasts who were not to be trusted. Jesus asks us to go out from what is most familiar and comfortable to be with those who are marginalized. As a catechetical leader, your ministry often leads you outward from Jerusalem to Judea and Samaria as you encounter children and adults from all backgrounds, faith journeys, and cultures.

For Reflection and Discussion

- Am I comfortable seeing myself as an evangelizer?
- What areas of evangelization am I most gifted in? What are my weak areas?
- How do I now view the relationship between evangelization and catechesis? What implications does this have for my ministry?

Growing as a Catechetical Leader

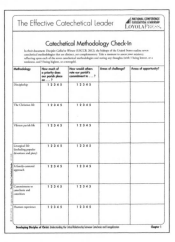

"The Church in America must speak increasingly of Jesus Christ, the human face of God and the divine face of man," writes Pope Saint John Paul II. "It is this proclamation that truly makes an impact on people, awakens and transforms hearts, in a word, converts. Christ must be proclaimed with joy and conviction, but above all by the witness of each one's life" (*Ecclesia in America*, #67). As catechetical leaders, it is important that we speak not just *about* Jesus but *to* Jesus. Many young people live in homes where they are not practicing their faith. Our witness to the Good News might be the only gospel some young people encounter. As you consider your ministry, what would those you minister to "read" in your life about the face of Jesus Christ?

Go to www.loyolapress.com/ECL to access the worksheet.

Suggested Action

"I invite Christians, everywhere, at this moment, to a renewed personal encounter with Jesus Christ, or at least openness to letting him encounter them; I ask all of you to do this unfailingly each day" (Pope Francis, *Evangelii Gaudium, The Joy of the Gospel*, #3). There are many ways in which we can encounter Christ. Set aside some time every day to encounter Christ. Suggestions include: praying, reading Scripture, performing a spiritual or corporal act of mercy, or setting aside time every day to pray in the church where you minister. Pray that God will help you recognize unexpected encounters with Christ every day.

For Further Consideration

Evangelii Nuntiandi (On Evangelization in the Modern World). Pope Paul VI (Boston: Pauline Media, 1976).

Evangelii Gaudium: Apostolic Exhortation on the Proclamation of the Gospel in Today's World. Pope Francis (Washington, DC: United States Conference of Catholic Bishops, 2013).

Go and Make Disciples: A National Plan and Strategy for Catholic Evangelization in the United States (Washington, DC: United States Conference of Catholic Bishops, 1992, 2002).

Disciples Called to Witness: The New Evangelization (Washington, DC: United States Conference of Catholic Bishops, 2012).

2

New Times Call for New Ways:
The New Evangelization

Evangelization: Not a Passing Trend

Evangelization and catechesis are the means by which the Catholic Church passes on the faith from one generation to the next. The call to evangelize is not a passing trend in the church but has been part and parcel of the work of the church for two thousand years. Since evangelization isn't new, you might feel confused by the term *New Evangelization*. You might also be wondering what it has to do with your role as a catechetical leader. What's so "new" about the New Evangelization, and why is the Church today emphasizing its necessity as never before?

Before we answer these questions, it might be helpful here to trace a brief historical narrative of how evangelization has shaped our world. Doing so will take us up to the current day and help us see why a New Evangelization is urgently needed.

The Historical Four Waves of Evangelization

In his book *Navigating the New Evangelization* (Jamaica Plain, MA: Pauline Books, 2014), Father Raniero Cantalamessa outlines what he calls the "four waves of evangelization." He identifies the protagonists (or leading characters) of each major evangelization initiative throughout the world and how they engaged in evangelization. Using the format of *when*, *who*, and *how*, let's take a brief look at these four waves.

The First Wave of Evangelization

When: the first through third centuries, during which large parts of the Roman Empire were converted

Who: chiefly the Apostles, followed by the bishops

How: The first several decades of this wave of evangelization are recorded in the Acts of the Apostles as a response to concrete historical events. The missionary activity of the Apostles was fueled by their personal encounters with Jesus. They proclaimed the Jesus with whom they lived, spoke, and walked for three years and for whom they were willing to die. From the middle of the first century onward, evangelization became more organized and codified by the local Christian community under the direction of the bishop as a response to various heresies, or denials of one or more truths of the faith, that began to emerge in the Christian world.

The Second Wave of Evangelization

When: the fourth through ninth centuries, during which the faith was spread throughout Europe following the so-called barbarian invasions

Who: the monks

How: Culturally and intellectually, the Greek and Roman peoples regarded the "barbarians"—the Germanic and Slavic peoples of northern Europe—as inferior to them. Gradually, Christians began to view these populations as a new mission field—particularly with the help of Saint Augustine, who saw them as brothers and sisters in Christ. Christianity changed from existing within a culturally developed and unified world to one in which there was no unifying culture or worldview. The rapidity and growth that characterized the church during this time were made possible because of a boldness and willingness to take steps beyond what was familiar and known.

The Third Wave of Evangelization

When: the sixteenth century, during which the "New World" was discovered and its inhabitants converted to Christianity

Who: the friars of Europe, including the Dominicans, the Franciscans, and the Jesuits

How: In the midst of the Protestant Reformation, Europe was becoming visibly and institutionally divided. The "New World" was a frontier for evangelization that seemed to have infinite possibilities. The goal of the missionaries during this time was to baptize as many people as possible for Christ, and pastoral care and inculturation of the faith were often neglected. Sacramentalization was prized above evangelization.

The Fourth Wave of Evangelization

This wave is taking place in the current era as the church engages in the re-evangelization of the secular West. Since we ourselves are a part of this movement, let's look at the New Evangelization in detail.

What's "New" about the New Evangelization?

The term *New Evangelization* was coined by Pope Saint John Paul II while speaking to the Latin American bishops in 1983 but was echoed and deepened by Pope Benedict XVI and Pope Francis. The term has left some Catholics scratching their heads, however, especially when we consider the reminder from Pope Saint John Paul II that "evangelization cannot be new in its content since its very theme is always the one gospel given in Jesus Christ" ("The Task of the Latin American Bishops," 1983). If the theme and the content of evangelization have

not changed in two thousand years, why do we need a "new" evangelization, and what is new about it?

There are three things that are decidedly "new" about the New
Evangelization.

1. the world in which we live

2. the audience and leading characters (or protagonists) of the New
   Evangelization

3. the way that we must preach the gospel—with new dynamism,
   new methods, and new expressions

Let's take a look at each area in turn.

A Whole New World

True story. As part of an interview for a catechetical leadership position, a candidate was asked, "Why do we need a new evangelization?"
The person replied, "I'm not sure. Maybe because the old one doesn't
work anymore?!" I had a bit of a chuckle about this later on!

When you consider the spread of Catholic Christianity throughout
the world, it is evident that we as a Church have been remarkably successful in bringing the Gospel to every continent.

Today, however, we are faced with a world less receptive to organized religion. We live in what has been called a postmodern secular
age. In his book *A Secular Age* (Cambridge, MA: Harvard University Press, 2007), Charles Taylor indicates that we have moved from
a time when it was virtually impossible not to believe in God, to
one in which faith, even for a believer, is considered one possibility among many others. Our world, Taylor argues, is characterized
not by the absence of belief or religion (although religious practice
has declined) but rather by the multiplicity of new options—spiritual
but not religious, nonreligious, anti-religious—by which people try
to make sense of their lives. While we can look to the lessons of

the past, we must also recognize that we are living in a new age, one characterized by the rapid rise in numbers of those who profess no religious identity, those who are formal members of faith communities but do not practice their faith, and those who have some connection to their faith but one that is tenuous.

The Audiences of the New Evangelization

The Center for Applied Research in the Apostolate (CARA) and the Pew Forum on Religion and Public Life provided valuable data regarding the changing face of the Catholic Church. Key findings from the Pew Forum in 2015 help us to identify how our audience is changing.

- Nearly a third of all U.S. adults (31.7 percent) were raised Catholic, and most of them continue to identify as Catholics today.
- The median age of Catholic adults is 49 years of age. This is up from 45 in 2007.
- Since 2007, there has been a 3-percent decline in the number of Americans who identify as Catholic.
- Nearly 13 percent of all Americans are former Catholics—people who no longer identify with the faith, despite having been raised in the Catholic Church.
- Two percent of Americans are converts to Catholicism.
- Sixteen percent of millennials identify as Catholic, the lowest religiously-affiliated generation in the history of Catholicism.
- As an overall share of the population, Catholics are declining, from 23.9 percent of the adult population in 2007 to about 20.8 percent in 2015.

The biggest implication of these statistics for you as a catechetical leader and for all pastoral ministers is that Catholicism can no longer be seen as a homogenous group whose members hold all the teachings

So true!

of the Catholic Church in common. When people say they are Catholic, what we think they mean and what they actually do mean may be completely different. In her book *Forming Intentional Disciples* (Our Sunday Visitor, 2012), Sherry Weddell urges us never to accept a label in place of a story. When someone says she is Catholic, this may mean that she attends Mass daily or once a month or only on Christmas or Easter. For others, it might mean they no longer go to Mass but still want to be married in the Church or have their child baptized. We can no longer assume that Catholic beliefs and practices are expressed in the way they once were!

Consider a group over which much ink has been spilled—the so-called *nones*, those who indicate "none" when asked to identify their religious affiliation. The nones presently account for one in five of the general population and are a growing demographic. We mistakenly assume that these individuals have made a fixed decision about faith, but nothing could be further from the truth. "None" is not akin to "nonbelief," if the Pew Forum Research of 2012 is any indication. For example, 94 percent of the unaffiliated believe in God, and 49 percent of those believe in a personal God! Not only that, but 30 percent are formal members of religious communities. This means that in our parishes, people who would describe themselves as "nones" are likely sitting alongside people who go to Mass weekly and those who attend infrequently. "None" does not mean "Not Open to the New Evangelization"!

We have a duty and an obligation, by virtue of our baptism, to proclaim the gospel. With this in mind, Pope Francis and his predecessors have identified the following three audiences of the New Evangelization:

- ourselves
- those who are indifferent to or have rejected the gospel
- those who have never heard the gospel

- **Ourselves: First Things First!**

  At a meeting of the United States Conference of Catholic Bishops in 2012, Cardinal Timothy Dolan challenged the bishops with the following words: "First things first. . . . We cannot engage culture unless we let [Jesus] first engage us; we cannot dialogue with others unless we first dialogue with Him; we cannot challenge unless we first let Him challenge us." The New Evangelization begins with each one of us, with our own conversion and continued conversion to Jesus Christ. We cannot lead others to Jesus until we have gone to him ourselves. We ought not to evangelize others unless we have been evangelized, and we cannot disciple others effectively unless we are disciples. Every one of us, regardless of our vocation, role in life, or ministry, is called to holiness and to growth in the Catholic faith.

- **Those Who Are Indifferent to, or Have Rejected, the Gospel**

  "With Mass attendance rates hovering at around 30 percent in many dioceses, it is clear that the vast majority of Catholics are not practicing the outward expression of their faith. We live in a time," writes Saint John Paul II, "where entire groups of the baptized have lost a living sense of the faith, or even no longer consider themselves members of the Church, and live a life far removed from Christ and his Gospel. In this case, what is needed is a 'new evangelization' or a 're-evangelization' (*Redemptoris Missio*, #33)." Prophetic words indeed!

  Today, the mission field has shifted from foreign to domestic as we "re-propose" Jesus to those who have heard the basic proclamation of the life, Death, and Resurrection of Christ but mistakenly believe that it has nothing of value to offer them. Parishes report that Easter Sunday and Christmas Mass are the highest attended services of the year. As ministers, we have a whole litany of terms such as Chreasters and Eastmasses (for those who attend Mass at Christmas and Easter), PACErs (those who attend on Palm Sunday, Ash Wednesday, Christmas, and Easter), fallen-away Catholics, and cafeteria Catholics—all used to refer to a complex demographic that is in no way homogenous. This group may include our spouse, our children, our grandchildren, or our close friends. They may have left the Church because of a specific personal issue or simply drifted away from the regular practice of their faith. All of these groups constitute a ripe mission field for those in ministry.

- **"To the Ends of the Earth"**
  We cannot forget that evangelization must be concerned with preaching the gospel to those who do not know Jesus Christ. This audience of the New Evangelization constituted the largest share of missionary work in the past. We are a pilgrim people and a pilgrim church. Jesus calls us to be witnesses of the faith "to the ends of the earth" (Acts 1:8), and this mission territory has often been known as mission *ad gentes* (meaning "to the nations"). All persons have a right to hear and receive the gospel. Pope Francis reminds us in challenging language that "Christians have a duty to proclaim the Gospel message without excluding anyone" (*Evangelii Gaudium*, #15).

New Times Call for New Ways

I once went to visit a parish that was having difficulty working with its youth and was looking for some helpful insights. Midway through the meeting, I asked what catechetical materials they were using, since they had indicated that the youth were bored. They mentioned a resource I wasn't familiar with, so I asked if I could take a look at it. No wonder I hadn't heard of it—it was about forty years old!

If we want to move our people from minimal commitment to being on fire for their faith, then we must be bold, we must be creative, and we must take risks! A renewed emphasis on the Church's evangelizing mission is necessary in order to adapt the message to the people. Using the expression "new ardor, methods and expression" coined by Pope Saint John Paul II, the Church seeks to engage and reengage the culture using all the means at our disposal, including relationship building, formation, retreats, classes, and new and emerging technologies such as social media and digital ministry strategies.

Let's take a closer look at new ardor, new methods, and new expressions and what each one means for you as a catechetical leader.

New Ardor: God Is Not Dead!

During one of my philosophy classes in college, a discussion focused on Nietzsche's famous statement, "God is dead." Nietzsche's claim is that God is dead because we Christians have killed him. If you profess belief in God, then shouldn't your life attest to that belief? Far from trying to prove whether God exists or not, Nietzsche is reminding Christians that when they claim to be Christians and yet live their lives without any reference to God, God does not appear to live within them. While his statement sounds stark, Nietzsche makes a good point. We are told by God himself that he is "not of the dead, but of the living; for to him all of them are alive" (Luke 20:38).

But many today have lost a living connection to a loving and real God, a personal God. Pew research from 2008 shows that "only 40% of Catholics 18–29 were certain that it is possible to have a personal relationship with God, and only 34% of them reported being at Mass on a weekly basis" (*Forming Intentional Disciples*, 45).

Many today have never read sacred Scripture or encountered Christ through the beauty of the Mass. But as Catholics who immerse ourselves in the Word, we are called to *be* the Gospels to the world. The Scriptures are to be writ large in our lives so that everyone we meet encounters the love of Christ in *who* we are. A new fervor and excitement should characterize our ministries so that evangelization may be fruitful. We can no longer sit and wait for people to ring the doorbells of our parishes. Instead, we must go out and encounter them as missionaries of Christ.

New Methods: "Catch 'Em All"

During the summer of 2016, the game Pokémon Go launched and became the most downloaded game in the history of gaming and social media. An augmented reality game (combining the real world and the digital world), Pokémon Go invites players, or trainers, to "catch 'em all." What people "catch" are virtual Pokémon at various real locations—including many Catholic schools and churches—as determined by GPS coordinates and Google Maps. Churches and businesses across the country reported massive increases in their foot traffic as young people gathered at these places to play the game.

During this time, I received a call from a parish about Pokémon Go, and the conversation itself is a microcosm of how we approach evangelization. In essence, the parish staff reported that groups of teenagers were gathering on the church lawn to play the game, and they didn't know what to do about this. Picture the scenario: young people are voluntarily presenting themselves at our parishes, and we stare at them through our windows, unsure what to do!

The first step is to actually take a first step—away from our offices, to where people are. We must be nimble and flexible in employing new methodologies to engage people when they present themselves to us. We sometimes tend to shy away from being creative and taking a risk for fear of failure. It is easier to play it safe than to "put ourselves out there." But when you consider the experiences of the early church—particularly Saint Paul, who was imprisoned, shipwrecked, and beaten—getting out of our comfort zone is critical if we hope to reach people today.

In response to the Pokémon concern, we in the Diocese of Green Bay produced a primer for parishes, helping them to understand the challenges and the opportunities that Pokémon Go presents. Among the advice offered was how to welcome players to the parish, how to help parents understand the game, and how to keep children safe. Being at the forefront of these kinds of initiatives means that we can shape the conversation for parents and children rather than let the culture shape our young people's experiences. Employing new methods can be hard, but the results are worth it. In the words of Pokémon Go, go and "catch 'em all"—and make disciples of them!

New Expressions: The Times They Are A-Changin'!

Every generation finds new ways of expressing itself. How we dress changes, what we listen to changes, and how we relate to one another changes. Consider that not long ago, social media didn't exist—and yet today many people maintain online relationships without ever meeting face-to-face. Technology has literally changed the expression of our relationships. In the past, relationships often went public when one person asked another person on a date and both families became aware of the relationship. And the most public expression of a relationship, of course, is the public witness of marriage. Today, however, one of the most public expressions of a relationship is changing one's relationship status on Facebook!

If we do not use new expressions of Catholicism, we will be viewed as out of step with the character of life today. Pope Paul VI reminds us that "evangelization loses much of its force and effectiveness if it does not take into consideration the actual people to whom it is addressed, if it does not use their language, their signs and symbols, if it does not answer the questions they ask, and if it does not have an impact on their concrete life" (*Evangelii Nuntiandi*, #63). While the entire gospel message constitutes a harmony, there have been increasing efforts to emphasize a wider variety of issues such as the following:

- care of the Earth
- racism
- just wages and fair working conditions
- the effects of sin on social structures and oppression
- the interconnectedness of life issues, including abortion, euthanasia, capital punishment, drug addiction, immigration, and human trafficking

By addressing these issues, we can express the gospel effectively in a changing world.

In addition, the great flourishing of new and traditional ecclesial movements and apostolates such as FOCUS (the Fellowship of Catholic University Students), TEC (Teens Encounter Christ), and CRHP (Christ Renews His Parish) is a sign that the Holy Spirit is moving in the Catholic Church in exciting ways. The reinvigoration of small Christian communities since the Second Vatican Council is another healthy sign that the New Evangelization is adapting to the needs of our communities.

The expression of our catechesis is also changing. Rather than being solely concerned with the memorization of doctrinal formulations, catechists and catechetical leaders are exploring a wider variety of creative methodologies (such as using cell phones and iPads to access information from trusted Catholic online sites) to effectively engage learners with the gospel. Our world has changed, and our young people are looking for such new expressions of faith so that they can bridge the gap between faith and daily life. And yet in many parishes, we catechize our children the same way we've done it for the past fifty years. Our books might be different—they may have more depth and more supplementary information—but we still too often use a methodology that does not take into account the learning needs of young people today. The printable for this chapter offers some insights and tools that will help you keep new ardor, new methods, and new expressions at the heart of your ministry.

Summary: Have Gospel, Will Travel

For so the Lord has commanded us, saying,
"I have set you to be a light for the Gentiles,
*   so that you may bring salvation to the ends of the earth."* (Acts 13:47)

The Good News has something for everyone—regardless of race, background, education, or ethnicity. The gospel is portable, adaptable, and shareable. It has the ability to appeal to indigenous peoples in Papua New Guinea and single millennials in Tokyo. For two thousand years, the message and person of Christ have spoken to people all around the world. Notice the language used in the Scripture above. God doesn't ask us or invite us to be a light for the world but implores us to be a light. He knows that we can do it if we keep the lamp of love burning in our hearts. This is no time to be a wilting wallflower or a shrinking violet! The time of the New Evangelization is upon us, and it is our time to shine and to help others shine for Christ. As catechetical leaders, we are commanded to be lights burning brightly for all to see.

For Reflection and Discussion

- What do you see as your own "new" and essential contribution to the New Evangelization?
- What new expressions of Catholicism have emerged through your ministry?
- What characteristics do you think are essential in people who evangelize?

Growing as a Catechetical Leader

"The New Evangelization is the work of the whole Church—lay, ordained, and consecrated. It's about friends, family and co-workers reaching out to one another and proclaiming the truth of Christ using all available means—conversation, personal witness, media, and the vast array of intellectual and spiritual riches the Church has built up in her two-thousand-year history" (*Evangelizing Catholics: A Mission Manual for the New Evangelization*. Scott Hahn [Huntington, IN: Our Sunday Visitor, 2014], 13). As a catechetical leader it is important to connect with people outside of the four walls of our offices using all the means at our disposal, whether online or in person. What means do you typically employ to share the gospel? How can you go beyond what is familiar and comfortable to you? How can you grow in your understanding of new insights, new technologies, and newly emerging pastoral realities?

Go to www.loyolapress.com/ECL to access the worksheet.

Suggested Action

"The effort of the new evangelization faces two dangers: one is inertia, laziness, not doing anything and letting others do all the work; the other is launching into many busy but ultimately empty, human activities" (*Navigating the New Evangelization*. Raniero Cantalamessa, OFM Cap [Jamaica Plain, MA: Pauline Books, 2014], 24). Take a look at your calendar and review the number of activities, meetings, and events. Now count the one-on-one meetings you have scheduled with people who wish to grow in faith and are seeking your help. Notice any difference? What actions can you take to correct any imbalance?

For Further Consideration

Jesus the Evangelist: A Gospel Guide to the New Evangelization. Allan F. Wright (Cincinnati, OH: Franciscan Media, 2013).

Living as Missionary Disciples: A Resource for Evangelization (Washington, D.C.: United States Conference of Catholic Bishops, 2017).

New Evangelization: Passing on the Catholic Faith Today. Cardinal Donald W. Wuerl (Huntington, IN: Our Sunday Visitor, 2013).

Resources for the New Evangelization—The United States Conference of Catholic Bishops has a number of excellent pamphlets about various aspects of the New Evangelization, including family ministry and catechetical ministry. See www.usccb.org/beliefs-and-teachings/how-we-teach/ new-evangelization/toolkit/.

The National Conference for Catechetical Leadership. See www.nccl.org

3

The Kerygma—The "Who," "What," and "Why": What We Believe about Jesus and His Church

The Good News Is GOOD News!

I remember the day my sister told me that she was expecting her first baby. I wrapped her in a hug and squeezed her so hard she was breathless. My sister was going to have a child, and I would be an aunt! Shout it from the rooftops! Once she had given her permission to share the news publicly, I couldn't wait to tell all my friends. And that's just what I did—I told all my friends, some two or three times in my excitement and joy for this new child.

Every Sunday at Mass, we have the opportunity to hear Good News. And what is our response to this Good News? Let's practice. The priest or deacon says, "The Gospel of the Lord," and we respond, "Praise to you, Lord Jesus Christ." Good. Now I want you to think about the *way* we say, "Praise to you, Lord Jesus Christ." Can you hear the sound? The understated and vague muffle of a lukewarm Catholic response?

In the Gospels, we hear *Good* News. That's right, Good News. I don't know anyone who responds to good news with a sleepy mumble and a yawn! The Cubs win the World Series! Your friend passes an important exam! Your spouse gets a clean bill of health after a health scare! Can you feel the excitement? The joy? The desire to run out and share your good news with everybody? Yes, these are natural responses that should characterize our hearing of good news.

Good news is good news for a reason. When we hear the Word of God and say, "Praise to you, Lord Jesus Christ," we should be filled with a joy so contagious that it affects and infects others. In his book *Under the Influence* (Chicago: Loyola Press, 2014), Joe Paprocki reminds us that "ultimately, the goal of discipleship is contagion: 'infecting' others with the Good News through our words and actions" (139). This proclamation of Good News—or, to use a Greek term, the *kerygma*—must be situated at the heart of evangelization and catechesis and imbedded in every single parish event, experience, and ministry. Every single one.

So, where do we start? We start with the person of Jesus—the "who," "what," and "why" of our catechetical efforts.

Jesus: Not What the Church Teaches but Who the Church Lives

"But how do we know Jesus was an actual person and not just made up?" John, one of my tenth-grade students, asked. "I know what the Bible says, but do we have any other evidence?" As catechists we are often asked this kind of question, and it can catch us by surprise. The temptation when faced with a question like this is to offer a standard response such as, "Well, the Catholic Church teaches us that Jesus is the only beloved Son of God our Father." While certainly true, this approach is unlikely to satisfy the hunger behind the question.

"Would you die for something that you did not believe in?" I asked my tenth-grade class that evening. Not one said they would. When someone we love dies, we carry that person in our heart and bring him or her alive in our words as we share our memories with others.

"So imagine," I said to my class, "that you were at the scene of your friend's death. You witness with your own eyes the murder of one you love. Afterward, you rush out to share the life, death, and—unbelievable as it sounds—the resurrection of your friend with others. They look at you like you are crazy. Then one day, you are arrested and condemned to death because you have been telling everyone about your friend, a friend you knew personally. Would you have the courage to die for that truth, or would you lie and live out your days filled with bitterness and regret?"

The Apostles were faced with the choice of living out the message of Jesus every day and bringing him alive to others or denying him and living a lie. When I share with my students that all but one of the Apostles was violently killed—beheaded, stoned to death, crucified, and, in the case of Peter, crucified upside down—they are amazed. Why would the Apostles allow themselves to be martyred for Jesus rather than deny him? It would have been easier to deny Jesus and deny what they had seen. Because, as one of my students answered, "Jesus is really the way, the truth, and the life," just as it says in John 14:6. Bingo! This was a lesson that I would never forget, and neither would my students.

The Jesus that young people are presented with and the Jesus of the Gospels can be vastly different. Jesus was a radical. He preached a radical message. He lived a radical life. He made radical claims about himself and his Father in heaven. This is the Jesus that young people need to be challenged with and comforted by.

At a conference in Norfolk, Virginia, in 2014, preacher of the Pontifical Household, Father Raniero, reminded us that "people will not accept Jesus based on the word of the Church, but they will accept the Church based on the word of Jesus." Leading with the "who" of Jesus rather than the "what" of the Catholic Church is the first step in helping people come to a relationship with Christ. I didn't know it at the time, but I do now: this lesson with my tenth-grade students was a sharing of the core gospel message, which is called the kerygma.

Kerygma: Back to Basics

Kerygma, meaning "proclamation," comes from the Greek word *kerusso*, meaning "herald," or one who proclaims. As the Apostles began sharing their experience of Jesus Christ, they started with the basics of his life, Death, and Resurrection. They began with the Good News that, through Jesus, God had drawn near to his people. Gradually and only after people understood and accepted the basic message did they progress to a much fuller instruction or teaching (*didache*) in the faith. Quite a bit of time was devoted to initial proclamation in the early church and helping people to develop a relationship with the person of the Good News. In this way, Jesus is both the message and the messenger.

Many today have not heard the Good News or may have heard bits and pieces of the Christian story but have not accepted it fully. They seem to get lost in the labyrinthine complexity of the teachings and doctrines of the Church and, to use a popular expression, "miss the forest for the trees." A back-to-basics approach is needed now more than ever, and it cannot be a one-size-fits-all approach.

From the lips of the Apostles the splendid simplicity of the kerygma was boldly proclaimed to different audiences in ways that were tailored to their receptivity, their background, and their standing in the community. We, too, are called to proclaim the Good News with courage and conviction as those who know and love Jesus. Even though the term *kerygma* might be new for us, we are immersed in the proclamation of the Good News regularly. For instance, in the Creed we proclaim at Mass, we regularly summarize the core of the kerygma:

For us men and for our salvation he came down from heaven: and by the Holy Spirit was incarnate of the Virgin Mary, and was made man.

   For our sake he was crucified under Pontius Pilate; he suffered death and was buried. On the third day he rose again in accordance with the Scriptures; he ascended into heaven and is seated at the right hand of the Father.

Let's take a look at the kerygma and some basic recipes that can be shared.

The Kerygmatic Process

If the kerygma is to be imbedded into all our evangelization and catechetical efforts, what is the best formula to use? The short answer is that there isn't a foolproof kerygmatic process that can be replicated exactly. The architecture of the kerygma depends on the audience. But in its most basic form, the kerygma contains five essential movements: creation, fall, redemption, re-creation, and salvation.

1. **Creation.** A loving God created the world, and each one of us is created to be in relationship with him.

2. **Fall.** Through humanity, sin entered the world, and our perfect union with God was broken.

3. **Redemption.** God sent his beloved son, Jesus, to redeem humanity. Jesus' life, Death, and Resurrection atone for the sins of the world. We are offered a share in this redemption.

4. **Re-creation.** From his position as Messiah, Jesus rules all things, and we are created anew through his life, Death, Resurrection, and Ascension.

5. **Salvation.** Belief in Jesus Christ and the Father who sent him is necessary in order to be saved. The presence of the Holy Spirit is a gift of the Father to his beloved children.

The vast majority of Catholics have some idea of the basic gospel story but need to hear the kerygma many times for it to take root. Some might be familiar with one of the movements but not all of them. Some people will need a slightly different or longer version of the kerygma, such as "the Great Story" in nine acts presented in *Forming Intentional Disciples*:

1. **The Kingdom:** an invitation to live in a reality in which God's will reigns

2. **Jesus, Face of the Kingdom:** an invitation to know the Person who embodies the kingdom

3. **Jesus, the Kingdom in Word and Deed:** the work of the kingdom—healing, forgiving, proclaiming, and teaching

4. **Jesus Embraces the Cross:** the mystery of dying as the key to eternal life

5. **Resurrection, Ascension, New Life, Adoption, and the Kingdom:** the victory over sin and death

6. **Jesus Asks Me to Follow Him:** an invitation to adopt this new way of living known as discipleship

7. **Personal Sin and Forgiveness:** transformation of the way we live

8. **Dropping the Net:** making a firm commitment to Christ and his body, the Church.

9. **The Life of Discipleship:** waking up each day to a new way of living

Regardless of the format that you use, it is important for you to be thoroughly familiar with the kerygma before you introduce it to others. In addition to your own familiarity, the following are some important considerations to keep in mind:

- **Construct wisely.** The architecture of the kerygma depends on the audience, the maturity, and the degree of receptivity of the hearers. Spend time thinking about which movement of the kerygma the person(s) might be familiar or unfamiliar with and what their response to the story has been up to this point in their life.

- **It is what it is.** Proclamation is proclamation. It is not intended to be full catechesis, nor is its goal to get someone to "come back to Mass." Allow the power of the kerygma to touch the person's heart without unnecessary explanation.

- **K.I.S.S.** Keep It Simple, Sweetie. Introduce the kerygma using simple but powerful statements. Avoid lengthy exegesis and commentary.

- **Watch terminology.** We have a whole host of terms that we use in the Catholic Church that can be off-putting or confusing. Say what you mean, and mean what you say. Define what is meant by terms such as *Resurrection* or *Ascension*. Don't assume the person knows what these terms mean.

- **Easy does it.** If you think that your audience is switching off, take a break and come back to it again later.

- **Reflect and repeat.** The average person needs to hear the kerygma more than once so that he or she can grasp the significance of the message, reflect on it, and internalize it. Repeat the kerygma in different ways at different times.

- **Pray.** Begin your presentation of the kerygma with prayer. Prayer before, during, and after the process is not optional.

- **Be patiently pastoral.** Making a conscious decision to follow Jesus can be a very painful experience for some people. Being patient and loving during the process is critical.

- **Touch base.** Don't leave people hanging. Follow up later with a conversation and clarify or go deeper.

Kerygma Challenge: Make It Personal

Personalizing the gospel message can be a powerful experience for people. It moves them from seeing the gospel as something that happened outside of themselves to seeing it as something they participate in. The following format may help people personally connect to the Gospel story:

- A loving God created me for relationship with him.
- I have broken my relationship with God through my sin.
- Jesus restores my relationship with God through his life, Death, and Resurrection.
- Jesus invites me to trust him, to turn from sin, and to give my life to him.
- Jesus has poured the Holy Spirit into my heart to bring me to new life in his church and sends his church on mission so that others can experience that new life.

I have presented the kerygma in a ten-minute conversation and over a daylong retreat. Once you are familiar with the movements, you can adapt it as necessary. The printable at the end of the chapter provides an overview of what the framework for a kerygmatic experience could look like at your parish. There is plenty of room for adaptation, but the format works equally well for a ninety-minute experience or a daylong retreat.

I Was. God Did. I Am.

The New Evangelization and the kerygma are not about behavior modification or getting people to join a parish. Instead, they are about effecting conversion in the life of every person we encounter and walking with him or her on the journey to Christ. Joining a parish comes later—often much later—for many people. Conversion, or *metanoia*, involves a sincere transformation of mind and heart to the person and mission of Christ. It means turning away from one thing in order to turn toward something else. The *Catechism of the Catholic Church* outlines two conversions that happen in our lives.

1. The first and most fundamental conversion happens during the sacrament of baptism (*CCC* #1427). Baptismal profession is the foundation of our spiritual house.

2. The second conversion happens throughout our lives and is a task for the whole church to facilitate. Saint Peter's conversion after his denial of Christ is an example of this kind of conversion (*CCC* #1428, 1429). This conversion may be a "wow" moment or a series of smaller movements over time.

Conversion is difficult and often painful. Saint Peter wept openly at his denial of Christ. And at a conference I once attended, I met a lady named Shirley who summed up the kerygma through three major movements in her life: her life before she had a relationship with Christ and was living in a way not in harmony with the gospel; her life during a time of great suffering as a result of her choices, when she felt the love and mercy of God touch her heart; and her life afterward. She summed up her story: "I was (a mess). God did (what he did). I am (a new creation)." Then she sat down. It was succinct, authentic, and powerful.

Build a Bridge and Get Over It

In "Treatise of Divine Providence," part 1 of her *Dialogue*, Saint Catherine of Siena frequently uses the metaphor of a bridge to describe our relationship with God. Christ is the bridge that unites us to God across the chasm of sin, which she portrays as a raging river that tries to carry us away. The bridge represents our crossing from the darkness of sin to the light of Christ.

Interestingly, this image of Christ as a bridge builder has been taken up in the evangelical world and used as a means of conveying the gospel to bring people to conversion. The framework below is one means of illustrating the gospel and can be used effectively with the basic kerygmatic formula outlined in this chapter.

The Kerygma: The Heart That Matters

The expression "An arrow that is aimed at the head will not pierce the heart" helps us understand the intimate relationship between evangelization and catechesis. The kerygma is the arrow that pierces the heart of the seeker of Christ. Without the kerygma, our catechesis will not be effective or bear fruit. Pope Francis often speaks of the role of the kerygma in the catechetical process: "In catechesis too, we have rediscovered the fundamental role of the first announcement or kerygma, which needs to be the centre of all evangelizing activity and all efforts at Church renewal. The kerygma is trinitarian. . . . On the lips of the catechist the first proclamation must ring out over and over: 'Jesus Christ loves you; he gave his life to save you; and now he is living at your side every day to enlighten, strengthen and free you'" (*Evangelii Gaudium*, #164).

A catechist from Nigeria once told me, "You are so blessed in the Western world with all of your attractively presented materials and resources. These materials would be a tremendous help to us. And yet, it is a wonder with all of this that the Western world is not full of disciples." I was profoundly struck by his comment and asked him what he used to evangelize and catechize people in his diocese. "We have two things," he said. "We have the love of Jesus Christ alive in our hearts, and we have the Creed. That's it." That is it! A faithful witness coupled with basic proclamation is the best catalyst for growth in the spiritual life, as expressed in this excerpt:

"The subject of proclamation is Christ who was crucified, died, and is risen: through him is accomplished our full and authentic liberation from evil, sin and death; through him God bestows 'new life' that is divine and eternal. This is the 'Good News' which changes man and his history, and which all peoples have a right to hear." (*Redemptoris Missio*, #44)

As a catechetical leader, you are called to lead people more deeply into the kerygma, and the work of catechesis should reflect this. There is a tendency to think that initial proclamation is deficient because it is "too basic." This is not the case. The kerygma ought to elicit a response, in time transforming the hearer of the Word into a proclaimer of the Word and finally a doer of the Word. As such, the kerygma should constitute the centerpiece of all our evangelical and catechetical efforts. When people say, "Let's get to the heart of the matter," what they mean is that they want to go straight to the core and, once there, find that it is the heart that matters more than other matters. All else is peripheral. The kerygma is the heart of the matter and our point of departure for discipleship.

Summary: See, Go, and Tell

Now if Christ is proclaimed as raised from the dead, how can some of you say there is no resurrection of the dead? If there is no resurrection of the dead, then Christ has not been raised; and if Christ has not been raised, then our proclamation has been in vain and your faith has been in vain. (1 Cor. 15:12–14)

Jesus told Mary Magdalene to go to the disciples and tell them what she had seen, and yet some of the Apostles doubted her. Can you imagine the anguish and heartache she must have felt? Eventually, however, the Apostles came to believe her. Because Mary Magdalene believed and shared the Good News, we, too, share in this belief. We, too, are witnesses to the Resurrection.

There are many today who have lost a living sense of faith. They doubt believers and sometimes ridicule and condemn them. Mary Magdalene's tenacity and courageous witness remind us that at the heart of our faith is a relationship with a living person, Jesus Christ, the Son of God, who wants us to share him with the world. As catechetical leaders in the New Evangelization, we are asked to announce that we, too, have "seen the Lord" and to go and tell it to the ends of the earth!

For Reflection and Discussion

- How familiar am I with the kerygma?
- How do I facilitate conversion in my ministry?
- How do I help my catechists proclaim the kerygma in their classes?

Growing as a Catechetical Leader

"The *kerygma* is not simply a stage, but [the recurring theme] of a process that culminates in the maturity of the disciple of Jesus Christ. Without the *kerygma*, the other aspects of this process are condemned to sterility, with hearts not truly converted to the Lord. Only out of the *kerygma* does the possibility of a true Christian initiation occur. Hence, the Church should have it present in all its actions." (*Aparecida Document*, #278a). The kerygma is at the heart of the catechetical process. But is it also at the heart of our lives as catechetical leaders? In the coming days, reflect on the movements of the kerygma. Note any areas where

there is resistance or where you feel that you "know" the story and find it boring or trite. God often uses our weakness or resistance to show us where growth is needed. Practice sharing the basic story in your own words by telling it in simple terms to someone you love. Then, think of someone who might not be familiar with the kerygma. How might you present it to this person?

Go to www.loyolapress.com/ECL to access the worksheet.

Suggested Action

"I believe in Christianity as I believe that the Sun has risen, not only because I see it, but because by it I see everything else" (C. S. Lewis, "Is Theology Poetry?" in *The Weight of Glory*, 141). The sun rises and sets each day, regardless of whether we notice it. Is there a teaching or practice of your faith that you take for granted or one that leaves you cold? Make a list of three ways that you could recover a sense of warmth and energy for this aspect of your faith.

For Further Consideration

The Aparecida Document. V General Conference of the Bishops of Latin America and the Caribbean (CELAM) (2007).

Under the Influence of Jesus: The Transforming Experience of Encountering Christ. Joe Paprocki (Chicago: Loyola Press, 2014).

"John Paul II and the New Evangelization: What Does It Mean?" Avery Dulles in *John Paul II and the New Evangelization*, ed. Ralph Martin and Peter Williamson (Cincinnati: Servant/St. Anthony Messenger Press, 2006).

"The Ministry of the Word: From Kerygma to Catechesis." Pierre-Andre Liege, OP, in *Sourcebook for Modern Catechetics* (Winona, MN: St. Mary's Press, 1983).

4

No More Sitting Around and Waiting: Evangelization, Discipleship, and Mission

Going through the Motions?

Kristin's grandmother was a faithful daily Mass-goer. When Kristin asked her grandmother why she went to Mass each day, she wasn't expecting this surprising response: "Because I was told to." When Kristin asked her grandmother if going to Mass brought her any joy, she responded that it didn't, it was simply her duty to show up and be there. This story illustrates a simple but important point. We can never assume that those who are active and participate in our parishes (even by going to daily Mass!) have a relationship with Christ and are living out their baptismal calling. How many of our parishioners are going through the motions just as Kristin's grandmother was? Way too many, if current statistics are to be believed.

For decades, the unspoken message to Catholics about what is expected of them has been "pray, pay, and obey." In his book *A Church on the Move: 52 Ways to Get Mission and Mercy in Motion* (Loyola Press, 2016, 70), Joe Paprocki proposes that we instead replace this minimalist approach with the admonition to "grow, go, and bestow!"—an attitude that expresses discipleship, not just minimal obligation.

- **Grow:** Parishioners are expected to grow in their faith.
- **Go:** Parishioners are expected to go into the world to share their faith.
- **Bestow:** Parishioners are expected to share their gifts with the faith community and the wider world.

The goal of evangelization and catechesis working together is to create disciples of Jesus Christ who go out on mission to share their faith with others. But what exactly is a disciple, and how do catechesis and evangelization work together in the process of discipleship? In this chapter we will explore what it means to live as a disciple of Christ in the New Evangelization and identify some of the ways evangelization and catechesis work together to form disciples sent on mission.

What Is a Disciple?

A disciple is one who follows Jesus, loves him, wants to learn from him, be with him, and share him with others. The entire discipleship process is an apprenticeship in faith, in the living out of the Christian life. This is a process that takes place over a lifetime, grows as we grow, and is shaped by our experiences of the world around us. Pope Francis reminds us that "being a disciple means being constantly ready to bring the love of Jesus to others, and this can happen unexpectedly and in any place: on the street, in a city square, during work, on a journey" (*Evangelii Gaudium*, #127). This can happen to us at the grocery store or on social media. I often describe disciples as being "tabernacles with feet" as they bring the Word of God to the world in their daily living.

We can no longer assume that those in our pews are evangelized, and we cannot sit around waiting for people to ring the doorbells of our parishes asking to be evangelized. Just because a church and its various ministries exist does not mean that discipleship is happening. One of my favorite quotes from Sherry Weddell's book *Forming Intentional Disciples* is from Father Damian Ference. He writes: "All too often those of us in positions of Church leadership assume that all folks in the pews on Sundays, all the children in our grade schools, high schools and . . . in our youth groups and all the members of our RCIA team are already disciples. Many are not. The same can be said of staffs and faculties of Catholic institutions. Our people may be very active in the programs of our parishes, schools and institutions but unfortunately, such participation does not qualify for discipleship" (55). This is a critical point. Just because people show up and may be active in our ministries and programs does not mean that they are disciples!(Active participation does not mean discipleship.) So, what are the instruments of a well-tuned disciple's life?

- **A Personal Relationship.** A disciple has a personal relationship with Jesus, can articulate it, and introduces others to Jesus.
- **Prayer.** A disciple prays regularly.
- **Commitment.** A disciple has a commitment to Jesus, his church, and the kingdom.
- **Worship.** A disciple worships regularly.
- **Study.** A disciple studies sacred Scripture and other Christian writings.
- **Openness.** A disciple is open to the Holy Spirit and to where the Lord is leading him or her.
- **Participation.** A disciple participates in the community and in the sacramental life of the church.
- **Service.** A disciple serves others in the name of Jesus Christ.
- **Generosity.** A disciple shares his or her personal gifts, time, and treasure with the Lord and his church.
- **Evangelization.** A disciple evangelizes the world through word and deed.

Some of these instruments may be developed together or in stages, depending on whether people are just beginning their discipleship journey or are further along. Understanding the roles of catechesis and evangelization and how they work together will help you be more mindful in your planning and in your approach to catechetical leadership.

First Things First: Follow the Leader

The word *disciple* comes from the Greek word *mathetes*, meaning a pupil or student of the master. The master is, of course, Jesus Christ. Jesus is the conductor of our ministry and our lives. In order to follow him, we need to be attentive and watch for his cues. Where he leads, we follow.

Jesus himself gives us a simple method of discipleship. What does Jesus do before choosing his disciples? He goes away to pray and to discern whom to choose in conversation with his Father. Throughout the Gospels, Jesus regularly retreats from the world to spend time alone in prayer. Prayer is at the heart of the disciple-making process. In ministry, we run the risk of spending our days talking about Jesus but not talking *to* him. Jesus' example shows us that taking every discipleship decision to the Father is the best first step.

How many times do we in ministry race into our day without pausing to spend time with the Lord? I often rush past the chapel in our Pastoral Center so that I can get right to the busy work of the day instead of taking the time to acknowledge the One from whom all grace flows. Time spent in prayer is never wasted. From prayer, we emerge in touch with God, often refreshed, strengthened, and renewed to minister. Prayer should be at the center of and permeate the entire evangelization and catechetical process. In *Navigating the New Evangelization*, Father Cantalamessa reminds us that "prayer is essential for Evangelization because Christian preaching is not primarily the communication of doctrine, but rather the communication of existence, of a life. The one who prays without speaking evangelizes more than the one who speaks without praying" (34).

The very life of Jesus constitutes a framework for the disciple-making process. Jesus had a process for forming disciples. He went away, often by himself, to pray and converse with his father. In the document "Living as Missionary Disciples: A Resource for the New Evangelization" from the USCCB the Bishops remark that "Christ gives us the method: 'Come and see' (Jn 1:46), 'Follow me' (Mt 9:9), 'Remain in me' (Jn 15:4), and 'Go, there- fore, and make disciples of all nations' (Mt 28:19)" (9). This corresponds to the terms encounter, accompany, community, and send which is the formative itinerary for missionary discipleship.

When the missionary discipleship process and the example of Jesus are united, the framework looks like this:

- "Come and see": Encounter
- "Follow me": Accompaniment
- "Remain united with me": Community
- "Go and make disciples": Mission

This framework is echoed very nicely in the stages of the evangelization process, which we will explore later in this book. Catechesis, for example, is most effective only after evangelization—when someone has had an encounter with Christ and is open to hearing more about who he is.

The Parish Symphony of Discipleship

Activity alone is no guarantee that discipleship is happening in a parish. Parishes may have a packed calendar, but very often these events and experiences are disjointed and end up becoming more of a distraction than an attraction. Everyone wants to have a vibrant parish, but vibrancy flows from spiritual growth rather than from busyness. In this section, we will explore the concept of discipleship from a parish perspective using the metaphor of a symphony orchestra. Orchestras can range from small chamber orchestras with fewer than fifty members to large symphony orchestras with more than one hundred members. Regardless of size, a great orchestra plays beautiful music because of some shared foundational principles. Let's take a look at some of the foundational principles of parish discipleship.

- **Intentionally Play Music Together**
  A buzzword today in the broader culture and in the church is *intentionality*. There are numerous blogs and Web sites devoted to "intentionally meaningful living" or "intentional simplicity," for example. As a church, intentionality should be at the center of our efforts to evangelize and catechize our parishioners. Working together to form youth, young adults, and adults takes a concerted effort and a common vision. It requires an ability to transcend the "turf wars" or "silo mentality" that we often see among parish staff who fall prey to the habit of conducting their ministries with tunnel vision focused on their own area.

  When one or more staff members adopt a "silo mentality," different ministries exist side by side but do not have reciprocity and integration in their vision and ministerial practices. Each ministry operates independently of the other, and there is little dialogue about true collaborative ministry practices or a shared vision. A side effect of this is the dreaded parish staff meeting where people gather, report on what they are doing independently of each other, and leave to go back to their own ministries. This situation has got to change. Every opportunity in the parish, including meetings—especially meetings—should have the making of disciples as a central aim.

  Why? Because the context for our ministry today is the New Evangelization, and the instrument of the New Evangelization is the disciple. If the goal of our work is to create disciples of Jesus, then we must design processes that foster a culture of discipleship within the parish. Having the entire parish staff and parish population on board is the key to avoiding the "silo mentality" syndrome. Rather than thinking of them as independent players on a stage, think instead of your pastoral staff as an orchestra in which each member of the team plays his or her own ministerial music but is in harmony with everyone else and with the overall mission and vision of the parish and the goal of making disciples. Everyone plays a different instrument, but only when the musicians share the same music and allow themselves to be conducted (by the Holy Spirit) does a symphony of beautiful music emerge!

- **Hallelujah Is Our Theme Song!**
While many people believe that worldwide membership of the Catholic Church is declining, the opposite is actually true. The Catholic Church is growing worldwide, and the number of baptized Catholics has grown at a faster rate than that of the world's population, according to the Vatican's Central Office for Church Statistics. The figures presented in the *Annuario Pontificio* 2016, the Vatican yearbook, and in the *Statistical Yearbook of the Church* give detailed statistics on the Church's workforce, sacramental life, dioceses, and parishes as of December 31, 2014. These figures are at odds with the depiction of a dying faith so often conjured by the media. But if the Church is actually growing worldwide, then why are Mass attendance rates hovering at around 30 percent nationally?

The problem lies in the fact that we are not making disciples. We have more programs, events, and resources than ever before, but in general there is a widespread disconnect between the teachings of the Church and the practice of the faith among Catholics, particularly when it comes to moral issues. Our problem is not one of attraction but one of retention. We cannot seem to keep Catholics engaged in the life of our parishes. In the United States we tend to do fairly well at attracting people to Catholicism, but we are hemorrhaging members from our parishes faster than any other denomination, according to Pew research from 2015. For every convert who comes into the American Catholic Church, six existing Catholics will leave. We have become, as one observer said to me, the church for the "hatch, match, and dispatch"! We see people, if at all, when they are hatched (baptism), when they find a match (marriage), and then when they are dispatched (funerals).

Although this is a cause for grave concern and an urgent matter, it should not lead to despair. The grace of God is always moving. As Pope Saint John Paul II reminds us over and over, we are an Easter people, and hallelujah is our song. So let's give our parish life a tune-up so that the piece we play is one that people will never forget and that sustains them for life!

Orchestrate Discipleship for the Benefit of All

In his book *Growing True Disciples* (Waterbrook, 2001), George Barna reports on extensive research conducted on congregations throughout the United States. He found a common pattern among all denominations: there were a plethora of programs offered in parishes but few intentional, systematic processes for discipleship and evangelization. When asked how they wanted to improve their discipleship programs, many church leaders said that they would develop a more clearly articulated plan or approach to discipleship focused on growth rather than the usual benchmarks and standards. Barna asks us, "What if we were to change our standards? Suppose we were to de-emphasize attendance statistics, square footage and income figures in favor of a commitment to depth and authenticity in discipleship?" (4). How would this mindset change our planning? How would we ensure that the spiritual norm in our parishes was not an inch deep and a mile wide but rather deep and expansive?

What we lack in most cases at the parish is a model of discipleship and an intentional and well-thought-out process for making disciples. We must give attention to formation processes that

- transform Catholics from being merely consumers of religious services to being disciples sent on mission.
- foster the disciplines of the Christian life, including prayer, study, almsgiving, fasting, and service.

Instead of focusing our ministries on strengthening our own area—such as youth ministry, schools, or stewardship—our focus should be discipleship. Strong youth participation, stewardship, service, and formation, it must be remembered, are all the fruits of discipleship.

Every parish needs to grapple with its capacity to evangelize and catechize people effectively. There is no one-size-fits-all approach and no magic bullet. What works well for one parish will not work for another. Like any orchestra, the music performed will be determined by the musicians and musical selections. Each parish must decide upon the music that it will play in order to form, inform, and transform its members.

Let's look at some of the components of the disciple-making process, beginning with the first and most important principle—following Jesus.

Mission On

During a pastoral council meeting, members were discussing endless ways to bring new members into their parish, which was declining in membership each year. The question was asked, "How do we get all those people out there to come in here?" I couldn't help but wonder if this question (which I have heard many times) was the right question to ask. What do you notice about the language used in the question and the way that it is framed? When I hear this question, I am struck by two things.

1. the "us versus them" mentality
2. the movement from "out there to in here"

The focus is on bringing "those" people in here to worship with us. Very often this question really means, "How do we get those people to come to Mass?" The missionary-oriented question, on the other hand, asks something different: "How do we get all the people in here to go out there and reach others for Christ?" The emphasis is on the going out and sending forth, and the people who are reached are our friends, our family members, and our neighbors.

Parishes will often begin the discipleship process by revamping their parish mission statement. During this process (which can take up to a year), many unnoticed members will leave the Church quietly and without telling us. Is this what mission has been reduced to—a new mission statement on the wall of an office or classroom that few will remember unless it is breathed into the life of the entire parish? One of the biggest revelations to me about the disciple-making process is that we are too often a people without a mission.

The truth is, we are a people who *are* a mission.

We often become ministers because of two things: our love for our Catholic faith and our love for others. God calls us and we respond. He leads, we follow. Jesus is the conductor. The parish is the orchestra. Our ministries are the instruments that work together to play music. Our song is one of discipleship for the good of his people. Mission is "at once a passion for Jesus and a passion for his people" (*Evangelii Gaudium*, #268).

In our ministries, we have the opportunity to form people for mission. People for others. People who transform cultures and change lives. We can walk with them and equip them with the skills they need to share their faith with the world in a credible and authentic way. We are equipping the next generation of saints in our disciple-making efforts!

Summary: It's the Pits

Can a blind person guide a blind person? Will not both fall into a pit? A disciple is not above the teacher, but everyone who is fully qualified will be like the teacher. (Luke 6:39–40)

What does Jesus do when a person falls into the "pit" of sin? He simply reaches into the pit and pulls the person out. Looking down, he doesn't focus on the darkness of the pit but instead calls the person to look up and into the light. This is what we are called to do as his disciples: to conform our hearts and minds ever more to Christ so that his love will shine through us to warm the hearts of those around us. If we keep our eyes closed and are blind to the world around us, we, too, will fall into our own pit.

In the discipleship process there is a principle that you can disciple someone only as far as you have gone in your own discipleship journey. No person is beneath our help. We are not called to lord it over others but to unite our joys and sufferings to the cross as we emulate the master teacher, Jesus Christ, who wants everyone to feel the warmth of his mercy and love.

For Reflection and Discussion

- What stages of the evangelization process do I spend most of my time on in my ministry? How is this a strength? How is this a weakness?

- When I consider my catechists, what stages of the evangelization process might they be most concerned with? How can I help them consider all aspects of the evangelization process?

- What is my understanding of mission? How can I incorporate a more missiological approach in my ministry?

Growing as a Catechetical Leader

We learned that there is a chasm the size of the Grand Canyon between the Church's sophisticated theology of the lay apostolate and the *lived* spiritual experience of the majority of our people. And this chasm has a name: *discipleship*. We learned that the majority of even "active" American Catholics are still at an early, essentially passive stage of spiritual development. We learned that our first need at the parish level isn't catechetical. Rather, our fundamental problem is that most of our people are not yet disciples. They will never be apostles until they have begun to follow Jesus Christ in the midst of his Church (*Forming Intentional Disciples,* 11).

As catechetical leaders, we minister to people at many different stages of the discipleship process and often forget our own journey of discipleship. We tend to focus more on others than on ourselves. As you reflect upon your own discipleship journey, would you say that you are in the beginning stage, the growing stage, or the advanced stage of discipleship? What reasons would you give for this?

Go to www.loyolapress.com/ECL to access the worksheet.

Suggested Action

The book *The ONE Thing: The Surprisingly Simple Truth behind Extraordinary Results* by Gary Keller and Jay Papasan outlines the *one* principle behind successful people that helps them achieve their dreams while living a simpler life. The authors pose an interesting question: *What's the one thing you can do that, by doing it, everything else will be easier or unnecessary?* As a catechetical leader, reflect on this question and write your one thing down. Pray about this, and ask the Lord to help you make this change.

For Further Consideration

Divine Renovation: Bringing Your Parish from Maintenance to Mission. James Mallon (New London, CT: Twenty-Third Publications, 2014).

Forming Intentional Disciples: The Path to Knowing and Following Jesus. Sherry Weddell (Huntington, IN: Our Sunday Visitor, 2012).

The Way of the Disciple. Erasmo Leiva-Merikakis (San Francisco: Ignatius Press, 2003).

5

Enter Catechesis: Catechesis as a Moment in Evangelization

An Apprenticeship into a Way of Life

As a catechetical leader, you no doubt want to have a solid understanding of the ministry of catechesis—which is too often understood as the transmission of information when, in reality, it is an apprenticeship into a way of life in the context of a relationship with Jesus Christ. Catechesis seeks to be transformative in helping people grow in relationship with Christ and his church. This chapter will provide a basic introduction to and understanding of catechesis as all the ways that the church forms disciples of Christ and continues to nurture them along the journey of faith. We will also outline the ministry of catechesis as presented to us in the *Catechism of the Catholic Church*, with an emphasis on the four pillars of our faith: creed, sacraments, morality, and prayer.

Instruction, Education, Formation: What Are We Talking About?

Through the years, the terms for catechetical ministry have changed.

- My mother-in-law tells me that she went to CCD (Confraternity of Christian Doctrine).

- My husband refers to religious instruction.
- When I worked at a parish, I was director of religious education.
- My children refer to faith formation.

Today, I hear many parish leaders refer to "evangelizing catechesis" or "conversion-centered catechesis," particularly when they speak of discipleship. Is it all "just semantics," or does it point to a shift in an understanding of the role, purpose, and nature of the ministry of catechesis? In my opinion, it is the latter.

Catechesis has become synonymous in most people's minds with religious education, or what once was called religious instruction. However, while religious education and catechesis are complementary, they are also distinct. The document titled *The Religious Dimension of Education in the Catholic School* (Congregation for Catholic Education, 1988) reminds us that there is a connection but also a distinction between religious instruction and catechesis. Catechesis is broader and deeper than education and instruction, but it encompasses both (#68). In *Catechesi Tradendae*, Pope Saint John Paul II gives the following description of the ministry of catechesis: "The name of catechesis was given to the whole of the efforts within the Church to make disciples, to help people to believe that Jesus is the Son of God, so that believing they might have life in his name, and to educate and instruct them in this life and thus build up the Body of Christ" (#1). Catechesis is a much richer process than intellectual formation and includes liturgical, spiritual, and moral formation.

Evangelization and Catechesis: Process and Moment

In her wisdom, the Church outlines for us the process of evangelization, which arises from the ministry of the Word, and describes catechesis as a "moment" within the process. "The 'moment' of catechesis is that which corresponds to the period in which conversion to Jesus Christ is formalized, and provides a basis for first adhering to him" (*GDC, #63*). A systematic and comprehensive process of faith formation that nurtures conversion includes the following five stages:

1. **Pre-evangelization:** This is the most passive stage of the process in terms of connection to any kind of formal religious affiliation. Those in this stage tend to have some link with the Catholic Church but are not actively practicing their faith. Many faith-formation parents, for example, are in this stage of pre-evangelization. They have some connection to Catholicism but have not consciously decided to follow Christ and go deeper. This stage builds upon basic human desires for security, love, friendship, and acceptance—desires that ultimately find their fulfillment in God. Fundamental questions of life are explored, such as, Why do I exist? Where does everything come from? Why is the world the way it is? What is my purpose in this world? Friendship, witness of life, and listening are appropriate pastoral methods to apply here.

2. **Initial proclamation of the gospel:** This is directed toward the following:

   - nonbelievers
   - those not practicing their faith
   - those of other religions
   - the children of Christians

   The kerygma constitutes the core work of this stage and aims to bring people to conversion. Often, the desire for initial proclamation may come after a significant life event when a person is more disposed to seek the face of God. Relating his or her experience to the gospel can be a powerful evangelizing moment.

3. **Initiatory catechesis:** Note that this stage comes after two preceding stages. This stage is directed toward

- those coming into the Church
- those completing initiation
- children and young people

It introduces, in a basic and evangelizing way, the life of faith, the liturgy, and the charity of the people of God. This is the "follow me" stage that Jesus invites us to.

Initial catechesis may come either before or after baptism. It is not uncommon to find young people who have missed faith formation for many years and have large gaps in their basic knowledge of the faith. As a result, catechesis during this stage often encompasses initial proclamation of the gospel, because conversion has not yet taken place. The hope is that the person may be led to a genuine profession of faith—which is the goal of this stage of catechesis. This is a time, especially for children, when the amount of information presented can be overwhelming. In all the documents of the Church, we are advised to take things slow and steady so that the basic and fundamental teachings of the Church can come to maturation. Skipping or giving this stage scant attention will lead to major problems later on.

Initiatory catechesis should

- direct the heart and mind to God.
- help people to participate in the liturgy, particularly the Eucharist.
- inspire an interest in missionary activity.
- nurture a Christ-centered life.
- nourish a Christian spiritual life.

- incorporate people into a community of faith that knows, lives, and celebrates the faith with them.

4. **Mystagogical or postbaptismal catechesis:** The Greek word *mystagogy* is roughly translated as "learning about or interpreting the mysteries." Mystagogy is the fourth stage of the Rite of Christian Initiation of Adults and extends throughout the Easter season until the feast of Pentecost and beyond. Mystagogy is not just for new members of the Church but for all of us. This ongoing formation, which takes place over a lifetime, is an initiation into God's self-revelation. It is a process of growing in the faith through prayer, learning, and practicing with other believers. In the section of the encyclical *Sacramentum Caritatis* titled "Mystagogical Catechesis," Pope Benedict XVI reminds us that mystagogy centers "on a vital and convincing encounter with Christ, as proclaimed by authentic witnesses. It is first and foremost the witness who introduces others to the mysteries" (#64). During this stage of the process, people are led even more deeply into the Christian life through the sacramental life of the Church, through prayer, and through becoming agents of missionary activity themselves. Remaining united with Jesus through the sacramental life of the Church is emphasized.

5. **Permanent or continuing catechesis:** Finally, and only at the end of the process, are people introduced to a systematic presentation of the truths of the faith. This stage is permanent, because it continues to nourish faith through deeper study and fosters continuous, ongoing conversion. Permanent catechesis is always concerned with missionary activity so that others can be invited into the process. Although catechesis enriches the life of people at every stage of their development, ongoing catechesis is oriented particularly to adult catechesis, which is a lifelong process. Ongoing catechesis includes a deeper understanding of the Scriptures, prayer, and liturgical and sacramental catechesis;

deeper spiritual formation; and a thorough examination of the Catholic Church's social teachings.

When I outlined these stages during a catechist in-service, one of the catechists approached me afterward. She said that she finally understood why her daughter would never read the life-changing book that she had given her or watch the eight-session DVD series that she found so interesting. She presumed that her daughter was at the stage of initial catechesis when she was still at the pre-evangelization stage. Now that she knew better, she would do better. She would adapt to where her daughter was in her journey and spend more time listening and walking with her rather than trying to teach her.

The printable for this chapter includes an overview of the stages and methodologies most appropriate for the particular audience of each stage of the process.

Aim to Get Intimate

The vision for catechesis is bound up with the missionary mandate of the church. As for the catechetical symphony we are conducting, the "sheet music" that we play from is centered on three essential movements.

1. intimacy with Christ
2. intimacy with the church
3. intimacy with the word

- **With Christ**

    In *Catechesi Tradendae*, Pope Saint John Paul II states that "the definitive aim of catechesis is to put people not only in touch but in communion, in intimacy with Jesus Christ: only He can lead us to the love of the Father in the Spirit and make us share in the life of the Holy Trinity" (*Catechesi Tradendae, On Catechesis in Our Time*, #5). The claim that catechesis should promote intimacy with Christ is a bold one; many of us may feel a little uncomfortable describing our relationship with Christ in this way. Part of our discomfort may arise because we associate intimacy with physical or sexual intimacy. But true intimacy is so much more. Emotional, physical, and spiritual intimacy are interconnected, and together they are at the heart of our relationships with one another and with Christ.

Unfortunately, intimacy is increasingly seen as something that can be bought, sold, and traded in our culture, especially among young people. Dating apps that promote the "hook-up" culture feed the consumerist mentality that it is perfectly acceptable to be sexually intimate with people we do not know. What has been branded as a quick way to become intimate with someone is clearly not intimacy at all.

By contrast, the Church teaches that intimacy is a sacred reality that grows and deepens gradually over time with much thoughtful work and attention. The same applies to our relationship with Jesus Christ: first we encounter him, and then we come to know him more deeply. As our relationship grows, so, too, does intimacy with him. This is the indispensable role that catechesis plays in the entire process of evangelization: it meets people where they are in their search for Christ and helps them come to a deeper understanding of who he is and what he is asking of them. Catechesis builds intimacy with Christ. There is no better way to become intimate with Jesus than through prayer and the sacraments. When our hearts are uplifted to God, there is no hiding from him: we are completely vulnerable and open to him.

• **Intimacy with the Church**
How many times have you heard someone say, "I don't need to go to church. I can talk to God on a hike in the woods or sitting by the lake"? There is something very beautiful at the heart of

this sentiment—that God can be present to us and accessible no matter where we are. This is certainly a big part of the Christian life, but it is not the only way—or even the most important way—to grow in our relationship with God. God has given to us the gift of a family in his church because he knows how much we need one another to live out the demands of the gospel.

We are not islands unto ourselves; instead, we belong to a continent of believers all across the world. Injustice, war, death, and famine affect all people, and "if one member suffers, all suffer together with it; if one member is honored, all rejoice together with it" (1 Cor. 12:26). God became intimate with his people in becoming one of us in Jesus Christ, who took on our flesh. It is true that you can speak to God wherever you choose, but there is no more intimate way to encounter God than in the Eucharist, which we celebrate with others. Jesus is most deeply and intimately made personal to us through his body, the Eucharist, and through his Mystical Body, the church.

The church, the people of God, is the realization of God's gift of communion to us in Christ. It is the natural environment for catechesis because it accomplishes the following:

1. provides the primary setting for the proclamation of the Good News

2. nourishes us in the Scriptures

3. welcomes and invites all who seek to love and know the Lord

4. facilitates conversion and discipleship

5. is the environment for the celebration of the sacraments

6. forms people for missionary witness in the world

7. gives form to missionary preaching that awakens faith

8. assists with early examinations and reasons for belief

9. communicates the essential elements of Christian living

10. instills a passion for the unity of all Christians

11. reminds us of the suffering borne by our persecuted brothers and sisters throughout the world

- **Intimacy with the Word**

My mother once called me to extoll the virtues of a particular book she was reading. "I can open it up anywhere, and it always has a way of speaking right to me," she said. I encouraged my mother to set down her book and go and find a Bible. When she came back, I asked her to say a little prayer and tell God what was heaviest on her heart and then to open the New Testament and read. The passage she read over the phone that day was from 2 Timothy 4:7: "I have fought the good fight, I have finished the race, I have kept the faith." For a woman who was struggling with cancer at the time, this message from God was a true gift for her. "I have never read the Bible this way before," my mother said to me. "Neither have I. We have never read the Bible together," I said.

For many Catholics who are searching or seeking, the Word of God offers comfort, healing, and hope. The Bible can affirm and uplift us but also challenge us. Get into the habit of reading the Bible each day, but when faced with a question or challenge, also consider opening up the Bible to the Psalms or the Gospels, for example. We can always find a way to bring the Word of God into everything that we do.

Revelation is how God speaks to us. It is God's self-disclosure to make known the mystery of his will and the invitation to share in his divine life. In creation and in the mystery of his Son, Jesus Christ, God is revealed to us in his Word, in the world, and in the church, through the Holy Spirit. Handing on this divine revelation is the principal work of the church. Sacred Tradition and sacred Scripture together constitute a single "deposit of faith," which is guarded by the magisterium, the teaching authority of the Church. It cannot be changed, since it comes from Christ himself. "Thus, the word of God, contained and transmitted in Sacred Scripture and Sacred Tradition and interpreted by the Magisterium, is the principal source of catechesis" (*NDC*, #18). Catechesis should always draw from Sacred Scripture and Tradition. They are our primary sources for the catechetical enterprise. Other sources that support catechesis include

- liturgical worship
- reflection on the Word of God
- the lives of the saints
- the witness of Christians
- social justice
- the promotion of moral gospel values

The Symphony of Faith: The Music of Catechesis

"So faith comes from what is heard, and what is heard comes through the word of Christ" (Rom. 10:17). These famous words of Saint Paul remind us of the responsibility of the church to hand on the teaching and practice of the faith. Each generation depends on the previous one to hand on the gifts of the faith. The music that carries parish life is not a single note but a symphony of teaching. Let's look at some of the essential "instruments" of this symphony—some key texts of our faith. As a catechetical leader, your familiarity with these "instruments" will help you create the beautiful music of the gospel in your parish.

General Directory for Catechesis

The Second Vatican Council mandated the development and publication of a comprehensive guide that would set forth the fundamental principles and organization of the Church's catechetical mission on behalf of children, young people, and adults. On August 11, 1997, Pope Saint John Paul II approved for publication the *General Directory for Catechesis* (*GDC*) as the norm and instrument for the Church in fulfilling her fundamental responsibility of teaching the faith. Setting forth the process of evangelization and the place of catechesis within that process, the *GDC* continues to be an indispensable tool for all engaged in catechetical ministry. As a companion to the *GDC*, the *National Directory for Catechesis* (*NDC*), published in 2005, builds upon the core themes of the *GDC*, including challenges to catechetical ministry in the United States, opportunities for growth, and the link between catechesis, evangelization, and liturgy. In many ways, the *GDC* and the *NDC* can be thought of as addressing the *how* of catechesis.

Catechism of the Catholic Church

The years following the Second Vatican Council saw an intense interest and flurry of activity in the ministry of catechesis, culminating in the publication of the *Catechism of the Catholic Church* (*CCC*) by Pope Saint John Paul II on October 11, 1992. The *CCC* is a comprehensive statement of the Church's faith and of Catholic doctrine attested to or illuminated by Scripture, the apostolic tradition, and the Church's magisterium for the entire universal church. It is not simply a doctrinal reference book but a collection of the truths of the faith. It includes the writings of the Church Fathers, the Doctors of the Church, and the saints of the church. Often referred to by Pope Saint John Paul II as the "symphony" of our faith, it is structured around four essential aspects of the Christian mystery, which we call the four pillars of the Catholic faith. In shorthand, these four pillars of the faith are sometimes referred to as the Creed, the Sacraments, Morality, and Prayer.

1. **The Creed—the Profession of Faith:** The belief in the triune God and his saving plan in Jesus Christ.

2. **The Sacraments—the Celebration of the Liturgy:** The celebration of Christ's saving action in the sacramental life.

3. **Morality—the Christian Way of Life:** A life lived in Christ.

4. **Prayer:** The expression of the Christian faith.

Reprise: The Catechetical Playlist

As a catechetical leader, you are part of a larger legacy of catechetical ministers that stretches all the way back to Christ himself, the master teacher. The task we have been entrusted with—sharing our Catholic faith with others—is a great privilege, responsibility, and gift. To do our job well as catechetical ministers, we need to balance and integrate three aspects of faith.

- "Who" we present (Jesus)
- "What" we present (content)
- "How" we present (methodology)

If we make sure these three aspects are always working together, those we evangelize and catechize will be touched deeply by the Good News.

One way to balance these aspects of the faith is to make and use a "playlist" of catechetical music. Such a list should always include certain "songs" in order to be considered complete. Your catechetical playlist, according to the *General Directory for Catechesis,* should

1. **Center on Jesus Christ.** At the center of catechesis and at the heart of evangelization is Jesus. Catechesis that is centered on the Person of Christ—that is, "Christocentric"—presents the gospel message as the word of God divinely revealed to human authors by the Holy Spirit.

2. **Focus on the Trinitarian dimension of the gospel message.** The source of the Christian message is the incarnate Word of God the Father—Jesus Christ—to the world, through the Holy Spirit.

3. **Proclaim the Good News of salvation and liberation from sin.**
The Good News of the kingdom of God includes the message of
forgiveness from sin.

4. **Flow from and lead to the church.** We are one faith, one
baptism, and one body, and we confess one God, who is Father
and Lord of all.

5. **Have a historical character.** Jesus and the events of his life are
historical realities that constitute a constant memory of the
church.

6. **Seek to inculturate the message to preserve its dignity and
purity.** The gospel is for all people in every age, in every culture.
Presenting the truths of the *Catechism* in different regions of the
world requires an adaptation of catechetical methods because of
differences in culture, age, spiritual maturity, and other social
conditions. Bringing the transformative power of the gospel to
all persons also means carefully preserving the gospel message.

7. **Respect the hierarchy of truths.** Different truths of the faith are
organized around central truths in Catholic doctrine and are
ordered accordingly.

8. **Emphasize the dignity of the human person.** Catechesis reveals
not only who God is but also who we are. In seeking meaning
for our own lives, we look to Christ, who communicated
profound love for each person.

9. **Foster a common language in the faith.** Familiar formulations
and prayers of the faith are necessary to pass along the faith from
one generation to the next and from person to person within a
culture.

Now that you have an essential playlist for catechesis—the "what" of
catechesis—we will turn our attention in the next chapter to the way
we present the faith—the "how" of catechesis. We will begin with the

"divine pedagogy," God's method of teaching his people, and then consider how we can use his teaching method in our own ministry.

Summary: Keep On, Keep Strong!

So let us not grow weary in doing what is right, for we will reap at harvest time, if we do not give up. (Gal. 6:9)

There are times when every catechetical leader has thought about giving up. The music of parish life can sound a bit out of tune at times. Our own ministries can become "one note" as we rotate through familiar lessons again and again. But remember, being a catechist and a catechetical leader is a vocation. God has called you to echo the love of Christ, the teachings of the Church, and the Word of God to the world. Sometimes our echoes are faint and discordant and sometimes they are strong and melodic. Behind you as a catechist are two thousand years of beautiful catechetical music that has touched people's hearts. Do not be afraid to play a different tune or sing a new song occasionally. The important thing is not to give up. Keep going, keep echoing for Christ!

For Reflection and Discussion

- Within the overall evangelization process, which areas need to be strengthened in my ministry? Which areas do I need to tune up?
- Are there areas of Church teaching I need to study more? Why?

Growing as a Catechetical Leader

"The most valuable gift that the Church can offer to the bewildered and restless world of our time is to form within it Christians who are confirmed in what is essential and who are humbly joyful in their faith" (*Catechesi Tradendae*, #61). In Jesus, the disciples encountered a joyful certainty coupled with obvious humility. Sometimes we take on too much in our ministry and end up feeling burned out. Sometimes we rely too much upon our own gifts and do not draw upon the talents of others. Take some time to reflect upon the words *joy* and *humility*. How can you become more humble and yet more joyful?

Go to www.loyolapress.com/ECL to access the worksheet.

Suggested Action

"Catechists are my favorite people. Why? Because catechists are intentional about their faith in a way that many Catholics are not. Catechists are very much aware of the call to live and preach the gospel in word and deed. Catechists are hungry to learn. Catechists are eager to get others excited about their faith in the same way that they are. And catechists like to have fun!" (*The Catechist's Journey*, Joe Paprocki, December 12, 2006). Catechetical leaders and catechists are excellent at foraging for spiritual nourishment—for themselves and for others. Think back to when you first became a catechetical leader. Can you remember the fire and hunger that you felt? Do you still feel this hunger today—particularly the hunger to learn? Identify two things that have robbed you of this hunger. What action will you undertake to minimize or eliminate these factors so that you can continue to indulge your love of learning?

For Further Consideration

General Directory for Catechesis. (Washington, DC: United States Conference of Catholic Bishops, 1998), chapter 2.

National Directory for Catechesis. (Washington, DC: United States Conference of Catholic Bishops, 2005), particularly nos. 15–25.

Catechesi Tradendae (On Catechesis in Our Time). Pope Saint John Paul II (Rome: Libreria Editrice Vaticana, 1979).

6

The "How" of Catechesis: Divine Pedagogy, Human Methodology, and the Six Tasks of Catechesis

"Mr. Talk and Chalk"

I had a college professor who spoke in a monotone voice, without inflection or animation. He would wish us a Merry Christmas in the same flat tone he used when he read the list of names on his roster! He never deviated from his script except to write a few words on the chalkboard, thus earning the nickname "Mr. Talk and Chalk." No matter how hard I tried to be attentive in his class, I struggled to stay awake.

As catechetical ministers, we can have the most dynamic and attractively packaged resources at our fingertips, but if we present the material in a dry and uninspiring way, we are unlikely to capture the hearts of our audience. When it comes to catechesis, content and methodology cannot be separated. As catechetical leaders, it is our responsibility to ensure that our catechists present their content both faithfully *and* effectively in order to engage those receiving it. In this chapter, we will explore what I call the "4, 8, and 6"—the four components of divine pedagogy, the eight effective methodologies that guide our catechetical efforts, and the six tasks of catechesis. That's a lot of numbers, so let's get going!

The Four Components of Divine Pedagogy

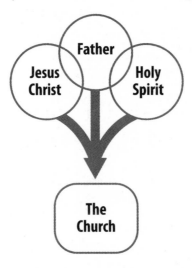

The word *pedagogy* comes from Greek and means "to lead the child." The way God speaks to us (revelation) constitutes its own pedagogy and methodology, which should in turn form, inform, and transform our own catechetical efforts. God reveals to us what we are to teach, how we are to receive this teaching, and how we as catechists are a part of this process we call "divine pedagogy."

What does the pedagogy of God look like, and how does it inform catechesis? The key to divine pedagogy is relationship: the relationship of the Father, the Son, and the Holy Spirit to one another. Through the loving communion of the Trinity, God reveals his plan to us—the salvation of each and every person—which serves as the source and model for all pedagogy of faith.

Here are the four components of divine pedagogy:

- **The Father: Creator and Artist**
  One of the first things we learn about in the Bible is that God is a creator and an artist. God created the earth from a formless void, and order was brought forth from the chaos of nothingness. The motivation for creation came from the very essence of God, which is goodness and love. God the Father entered into relationship with us through his eternal Word made flesh in Jesus Christ and through the act of creation. The ultimate manifestation or revelation of God's love is through his Son, Jesus Christ.

- **Jesus Christ: The Master Teacher**
  Jesus formed his disciples through his relationship with them: he prayed for them, called them and invited them to be with him, walked with them, shared stories with them, taught them, challenged them, and loved them. "He sent them out on missionary apprenticeship" (*GDC*, #137) in service to the world. Jesus' methods were diverse and multidimensional, depending on whether he was speaking to a crowd or to a single person. In his parables, he revealed complexities about the mystery of God and human nature. All means and methods—including natural ones such as the calming of the storm—were used to accomplish his redemptive mission. Fundamental traits of how Jesus taught include

  1. receiving others, especially the lost, the last, and the least.
  2. proclamation of the kingdom of God as the fullness of the truth and love of his Father.
  3. emphasis on the strong yet compassionate love of the Father, which promotes life and liberation from the bondage of sin.
  4. an invitation to new life sustained by faith in God and charity to one's neighbor.

5. use of all methods to engage people—silence, dialogue,
   metaphor, story, parable, and example.

- **The Holy Spirit: Wake Up, Shake Up!**
  The action of the Holy Spirit continues the pedagogy of God.
  The Holy Spirit is the one who enlivens and animates the church
  and directs her mission. As disciples, we are guided by the Holy
  Spirit, who remains with us and gives us the gifts that make it
  possible for us to live a new life in Christ. One cannot believe in
  Jesus Christ without sharing in his Spirit. It is the Holy Spirit
  who reveals to the world who Jesus is. Without the Holy Spirit,
  the divine animator, we would lack spirit: it is the Holy Spirit
  who wakes us up, shakes us up, and gives us the zeal and
  motivation to share our faith with the world.

- **The Church: A Loving Community**
  The church continues to employ God's own pedagogy and
  methods to form her members. Always seeking the most fruitful
  ways to announce the Good News, the church proposes and
  re-proposes the gospel but does not impose herself on any person
  or culture. The church seeks to engage the world for Christ and
  reflects God's own methodology for communicating the faith in
  a way that "is most appropriate to the circumstances of an
  ecclesial community or of those to whom catechesis is specifically
  addressed" (*GDC*, #118). The church herself is a living
  catechesis.

  Inspired by divine pedagogy, our catechetical efforts should
  focus on the following core methodologies:

  ○ Emphasizing God's love for each person, and his or her free
    response to God.
  ○ Accepting the progressive and gradual nature of revelation, the
    nature of the word of God, and its adaptation to differences in
    cultures and persons.

○ Placing Christ at the center of all catechetical efforts.

○ Valuing the community experience of faith.

○ Being rooted in interpersonal relations and the process of dialogue.

○ Using signs that link word and deed to teaching and experience.

○ Bearing witness to the truth and drawing power from the truth revealed by the Holy Spirit.

The church does not focus on any one human methodology over another; all work together to transmit both the content of the entire Christian message and the source of that message—the Triune God. One methodology is not more important than the other. My college professor could have used a variety of strategies to bring his class alive, such as storytelling, questions and answers, or multimedia, for example, but instead he chose to focus only on his preferred method of talking and writing on the chalkboard. As a result, his class was not as fruitful as it could have been. As ministers, we must use a variety of methods in our catechetical efforts rather than simply those that are most comfortable to us.

The Eight Elements of Human Methodology

The Church emphasizes eight elements of human methodology. Let's take a look at them.

1. **Human Experience**

   Jesus used ordinary experiences and images from everyday life—such as fishing, planting, growing, harvesting, and shepherding—to bridge complex concepts about the kingdom of God and the world. The most effective catechists do the same. When we learn something new, we start with our lived experience and bridge what is known to what is unknown. We try to make sense of the world around us by making associations between it and what is already familiar and real.

2. **Learning by Discipleship**

We learn to be disciples in our own time, place, and circumstances, but earlier disciples provide guidance. Our best and first model of discipleship is Mary. We look to her to see how we, too, can model complete surrender and abandon to the will of God.

Even the youngest members of the faith can emulate the example and real-life witness of good models. Catechists often ask if it is possible for children to become disciples. The answer is yes! While they don't often have the capacity to understand and articulate complex principles, they have "a unique ability to absorb and celebrate the most profound truths of the faith" (*NDC*, #29b). In the book *Dear Pope Francis* (Loyola Press, 2016), children from around the world ask Pope Francis questions and he responds. The questions posed show remarkable depth—for example, "My Mum is in heaven; will she grow angel wings?" and "How can you settle conflicts in the world?" These questions speak to a capacity for faith that is beyond what we adults sometimes imagine.

3. **The Witness of the Christian Community**

The vibrancy of catechesis and the vibrancy of a parish are linked to and depend upon each other. When a parish is lifeless, stagnant, and out of touch with people's needs, catechesis suffers. Parish communities must draw near to people and become key places where people can heal, discover Jesus, or rediscover him. Parishes are called to be a "sanctuary where the thirsty come to drink in the midst of their journey, and a [center] of constant missionary outreach" (*Evangelii Gaudium*, #28). How can your parish be a sanctuary of mercy, hope, and love where people who are thirsty and hungry can find food and drink?

4. **The Christian Family and Home**

   I serve as a lector at my parish, and one day as I was going up to read, I heard my three-year-old daughter call out, "Wait for me!" and felt her hand slip into mine. I was faced with two choices: (1) I could return her to her seat, thereby interrupting the flow of the Mass and risking a tantrum of epic proportions that would further disrupt the proceedings or (2) I could keep going and read with her beside me. I chose to keep going. As I was proclaiming the Scriptures, Ava remained quiet, and other than a discreet wave or two at some friends, she was well behaved. After the Mass, I went to Father and apologized for the situation. With a twinkle in his eye, he assured me that there was nothing to be sorry for. He reminded me that it is in such small witnesses that families and the church have transformed passive observers into active participants in the faith. This story reminds us that children naturally look to their parents, who are their first role models and witnesses of faith. It also challenges us to brainstorm new ways to assist parents in embracing this role.

5. **The Witness of the Catechist**

   Next to the home and the family, the catechist has a central place in every stage of the catechetical process. In our book *The Catechist's Backpack* (Loyola Press, 2015), Joe Paprocki and I remind catechists that "Our true calling is to live in the image of God who is, in essence, loving community: Father, Son, and Holy Spirit. In all that we do as catechists, our goal is to initiate and apprentice others into the life of the faith community. It is our responsibility, then, to know what the church teaches and has entrusted to us to transmit" (18). By our teaching and behavior, we speak of who we are and what we are about. Catechesis should echo the words of Jesus, who said, "My teaching is not mine but his who sent me" (John 7:16).

6. **Learning by Heart**

   From one generation to the next, the Catholic faith has been passed down orally, through story and sharing. For example, during the Penal Times in Ireland, which lasted from the early 1600s to the early 1800s, it was forbidden to practice the Catholic faith or to read or write books about Catholicism. During this painful time, the Irish relied upon memorization to pass along the faith. Even in situations that are not as extreme, Catholics rely on the memorization of certain formulations, prayers, and basic teachings, including factual information about the Church, parts of the Mass, and lists of the sacraments and the gifts of the Holy Spirit, for example. This learning by heart is a feature of living in a universal church and holds an important place in the catechetical process. We must never be so concerned with the memorization of information, however, that we forget that assimilation rather than regurgitation is the goal. Recitation of rote formulas can never replace understanding and conversion.

7. **Learning by Christian Living**

   If you devoured books about the sport of football but never played one game with a team, you could hardly call yourself a football player or a football expert. Practice is necessary for any discipline in life, and faith is no different. We learn our faith by living out our Christian faith. The private practice and the public witness of Christians are necessary so that we can live out our baptismal calling to sanctify the world. Catechists and catechetical leaders play an indispensable, important role in modeling what a lived relationship with Christ and the church looks like.

8. **Learning by Apprenticeship**

   In the early church, apprenticeship in faith was at the heart of the discipleship process. The *General Directory for Catechesis* states that catechesis is "an apprenticeship of the entire Christian life" (*GDC*, #67). Those coming into the early church were assigned a mentor, a master catechist, to guide them and walk with them. Readiness to become a full member of the church was gauged by both the master and the apprentice, without regard for the constraints of time. Master catechists aimed to balance the personal growth of the believer with the transmission of the Christian message. In the next chapter, we will look more comprehensively at the apprenticeship model of catechesis through the lens of the catechumenate process.

Now that we have explored the eight human methodologies, I would like to mention an additional strategy for evangelization and catechesis, one the U.S. bishops acknowledge as being tremendously important: the use of social communications technology.

"I Tweet, Therefore I Am."

Effective catechesis employs many different strategies to transform our parishes into evangelizing communities of lifelong discipleship. We must offer ample opportunities for youth and adults to understand what we believe and why, because other voices and forces within the secular world are influencing people to believe and act outside of the faith. One such powerful force is social media. It is shaping and changing our world, and many young people have no experience of the world outside it. Media and social communications have become an especially important tool for evangelization and catechesis and are not optional. Now, more than ever, we need to echo Christ in the media. Let's now talk about the work, or the actual tasks, of catechesis. Our catechetical efforts are inspired by how Jesus taught the disciples and how he helped them understand the different facets of the kingdom of God. Behind all our lesson plans, resources, and textbooks lies a framework that guides catechesis. To help our students develop into mature

Christian disciples, we must work within a unified framework that the bishops call the "six tasks of catechesis."

The Six Tasks of Catechesis

"All you have to do is provide information about the Catholic Church," a parent once said to a director of religious education named Amy. "I don't see how talking about issues of morality is important or helpful at faith formation; just teach them what they need to know," the parent said. While respecting the role of the parent as the primary educator of the faith, Amy informed the parent that there were six interrelated and complementary ways in which catechesis prepares students for Christian living. Conversion, like catechesis, is a lifelong journey, and the "six tasks" are dimensions of a life lived with Jesus. The more we know him, the more we love him; and the more we love him, the more we want to know him.

Here are the six tasks.

1. **Knowledge of the Faith**

   Many people think catechesis is only concerned with "book knowledge" of the faith. But this task is actually oriented toward the profession of and reflection on the Catholic faith, which is the content of God's revelation found in sacred Scripture and sacred tradition and lived out in the creed and in church doctrine. Knowledge of the faith is an expression of the church's living Tradition, which comes from Christ himself and is handed on by the apostles with the help of the Holy Spirit.

2. **Liturgy and Sacraments**

   Liturgical education includes not only teaching about the form and the meaning of sacraments and liturgical celebrations but also helping people to prepare their minds and hearts to enter into the mysteries of the faith.

3. **Missionary Witness**

   Mass concludes with the following options for dismissal, which make it quite clear that we are being sent forth on mission:

   - "Go forth, the Mass is ended."
   - "Go and announce the Gospel of the Lord."
   - "Go in peace, glorifying the Lord by your life."
   - "Go in peace."

   Our response is always the same: "Thanks be to God!" What else is there to do but to glorify and thank God, who sends us out to witness in our homes, our places of work, and our communities? The Mass ends—but it is then that our work in the world begins.

4. **Education in the Christian Community**

   Earlier we talked about the facts that "no man is an island" and that no Catholic is formed in a vacuum. Education for community life prepares people to live and participate in the life

and mission of the church—the Body of Christ and the
community of believers—as expressed in the church's origin,
history, and ecclesiology, and in the communion of saints and
their family, the domestic church. The example of Jesus and his
words "Just as I have loved you, you also should love one
another" (John 13:34) provide the method and inspiration for
formation in community life.

5. **Learning to Pray**

   The *General Directory for Catechesis* states that "when catechesis is
   permeated by a climate of prayer, the entire Christian life reaches
   its summit" (#85). Prayer is dialogue between a person and God
   and involves talking, listening, sharing, and wrestling with new
   insights and ideas. A healthy spiritual diet involves many
   different kinds of prayer.

6. **Moral Formation**

   The moral teaching of Jesus, which is the fulfillment of the
   commandments, means learning how to apply these teachings to
   our everyday lives. We are encouraged to develop a moral
   conscience that is conformed to Christ, informed by church
   teachings, and modeled in a conscientious life of virtue.

2, 4, 6, 8 . . . Who Do We Integrate?

This chapter has focused on the four components of divine pedagogy,
the six tasks of catechesis, and the eight human methodologies. You
might find your head spinning after reading much of this chapter!
Rather than see all these pieces as individual parts, however, concen-
trate on the essentials. Catechesis is modeled on God's own way of
speaking, and as a result, catechesis is multifaceted and prepares us for
our entire life. The chant "2, 4, 6, 8, who do we appreciate?" is often
sung by young people at the end of a sports event. Instead of merely

appreciating our faith and the gift of catechetical process, our song should be: "2, 4, 6, 8 . . . *who* do we integrate?"

Faith is so much more than appreciation and admiration; it is the integration of both a person and a message into our lives. At the heart of our faith is the mystery of relationship—a mystery that is embodied in the patterns of our liturgy. In the next chapter, we will explore how faith formation is better off taking its cues from the liturgy than from the world of academia.

Summary: Always Be Ready

Always be ready to make your defense to anyone who demands from you an accounting for the hope that is in you. (1 Pet. 3:15)

One principle we must remember in presenting the teachings of the Church is the principle of "clarity with charity." In its entirety, the well-known quote from Peter goes like this: "Always be ready to make your defense to anyone who demands from you an accounting for the hope that is in you; yet do it with gentleness and reverence" (1 Pet. 3:15–16). Gentleness and respect for the other person lie at the heart of all that we do as ministers. As catechetical leaders, we have many different methodologies at our disposal, and careful discernment is required in working with people at different places in their faith. What an awesome responsibility but also blessing we have been entrusted with!

For Reflection and Discussion

- When I look at the eight elements of human methodology, which of them best characterize my ministry? How could I become more well-rounded?
- Which of the six tasks of catechesis are at the heart of my ministry? Why? Which ones do I need to work on?

Growing as a Catechetical Leader

"Being a catechist is not a title, it is an attitude: abiding with him, and it lasts for a lifetime! It means abiding in the Lord's presence and letting ourselves be led by him. I ask you: How do you abide in the presence of the Lord?" (Address of Pope Francis to participants in the pilgrimage of catechists on the occasion of the Year of Faith and of the International Congress on Catechesis, Paul VI Audience Hall, September 27, 2013).

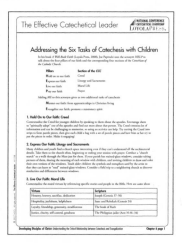

People who attend eucharistic adoration often speak of the peace that comes with sitting quietly in the presence of the Lord. But as we sit in silence, gazing at and adoring Jesus, so, too, he looks back at us. Sometimes we forget that eucharistic adoration is a two-way window, that what is seen goes both ways. If you haven't been to eucharistic adoration in some time, try attending this week. Think about what Jesus sees when he looks at you as his beloved child and as a catechetical leader.

Go to www.loyolapress.com/ECL to access the worksheet.

Suggested Action

"Faith for me isn't an argument, a catechism, a philosophical 'proof.' It is instead a lens, a way of experiencing life, and a willingness to act" (*Take This Bread: A Radical Conversion*, Ballantine Books, 2007, xvi). As you reflect upon your ministry, identify a catechist or child who seems to be struggling. What can you do to reach out to this person outside of normal class time? Could you send a card or a thoughtful e-mail? Could you deliver a meal to a family who is grieving or deliver flowers to one of your catechists who got a promotion at work? This week, choose someone to pray for, and then act upon your desire to affirm, uplift, or comfort that person.

For Further Consideration

Catechism of the Catholic Church and the Craft of Catechesis. Pierre de Cointet, Barbara Morgan, and Petroc Willey (San Francisco: Ignatius Press, 2008).

The Six Tasks of Catechesis: Key Principles for Forming Faith. Mary Kathleen Glavich, SND, (New London, CT: Twenty-Third Publications, 2016).

The Catechist's Backpack: Spiritual Essentials for the Journey. Joe Paprocki and Julianne Stanz (Chicago: Loyola Press, 2015).

The Way God Teaches: Catechesis and Divine Pedagogy. Joseph White (Huntington, IN: Our Sunday Visitor, 2014).

7

How Catechesis Should "Feel" and "Flow": Catechesis and the Catechumenate

The Master Mechanic and the Apprentice

My father is a mechanic, and when I was growing up, his garage was right next to our house. Through the years, we had ample time to watch him interact with his customers and see how he went about building his business. My brother Ian spent much of his childhood following Dad around the garage, carefully learning from my father as he patiently explained or demonstrated what needed to be repaired.

So it came as no surprise when my brother told us that he wanted to become a mechanic. He went to a technical college for the necessary coursework and then served as an apprentice to my father. Eventually he graduated and returned home to work side by side with Dad. When someone recently asked my father about my brother's involvement in the business, he responded that working on cars "was in the blood." In a way, this is true—but it is not the full story.

The real reason my brother became a mechanic is because of my father. In him, my brother saw a life lived well, in service to others. He overlooked the long hours of labor in a cold garage and saw instead a fulfilling and meaningful career built on relationship. My father taught my brother all that he knew, and today my brother is teaching his own son what was passed on to him. Without the witness of my father and this trade apprenticeship, my brother would not have become a mechanic.

In today's society, the apprenticeship model has too often gone ignored in favor of higher education. But there is value in both. College graduates often struggle to find jobs precisely because they don't have "on-the-job training." Employers want graduates who have a conceptual understanding of their job along with the knowledge and skills to perform it. In a similar way, it is important that we form Christians who not only have a solid understanding of their faith but also the ability to apply faith in everyday life. One of the best ways to do this is through an understanding of the process of Christian initiation.

The Catechumenate as Model and Guide

The catechumenate—the process by which people are initiated into the Catholic Church—serves to inspire all catechesis and is characterized by a "feel and flow"—a rhythm that takes its cues more from the liturgy than from the world of academia. The relationship in catechesis that imitates the catechumenate is not the teacher-student relationship but the mentor-apprentice one. The "Decree on Missionary Activity" describes the process as "not a mere expounding of doctrines and precepts, but a training period in the whole Christian life, and an apprenticeship duty drawn out, during which the disciples are joined to Christ their Teacher" (*Ad Gentes*, #14). Who, exactly, is the catechumenate for?

- Unbaptized adults preparing for full initiation through baptism, confirmation, and Eucharist.
- Those who have been baptized in non-Catholic, Christian denominations who have little catechesis and wish to come into full communion with the Catholic Church by making a profession of faith and receiving confirmation and Eucharist.

- Those who have been baptized Catholic but have never been catechized and need to complete initiation through confirmation and Eucharist.

- Those who have been baptized Catholic and confirmed as infants (in some countries this is the norm) but haven't received Eucharist.

- Unbaptized children who are at least seven years old. These children participate in a children's catechumenate or the Rite of Christian Initiation of Adults adapted for children. (There is no such thing as the Rite of Christian Initiation of Children.) Young people in mid- to late adolescence with a sense of maturity should participate in the RCIA process for adults.

The RCIA Is Not a Program

As a church, we need to retrieve the apprenticeship model and let go of the classroom model of catechesis. Too often, the catechumenate is seen as "one more program" in a long list of programs a parish offers. The catechumenate, in fact, is not a program at all but rather an ongoing process. This means that if someone who wants to become Catholic drops into our parishes in the middle of July, we are not to tell them they need to come back around the middle of September when our "RCIA program" begins. Likewise, the catechumenate is not accomplished by a single instructor providing instruction for catechumens but rather is facilitated by a team of catechists and sponsors. Finally, the RCIA should not be thought of as a series of classes following an academic calendar (typically September through May, when we "graduate" our new Christians). Rather, it is a process that is closely tied to the liturgical calendar and "begins" whenever someone "shows up."

Since Christian initiation is not a program but a process, it should serve the person rather than the other way around. In *The Way of Faith:*

A Field Guide to the RCIA Process (Twenty-Third Publications, 2008, 5–6), Nick Wagner offers a helpful list of what RCIA is not.

- It is not an adult confirmation program.
- It is not an adult education program.
- It is not a marriage preparation program, even if one person in the couple is not Catholic.
- It is not CCD for adult Catholics who "dropped out" after confirmation.
- It is not a place for sponsors or spouses to "catch up" on facts of the faith.
- It is not a small faith-sharing community.
- It is not a support group for dealing with emotional distress.
- It is not a class.
- It is not a club.
- It is not a program for making Protestants into Catholics.

So, what *is* the RCIA process? Let's take a look.

The Five Stages of the Catechumenate

Entering into a serious relationship with anyone takes time. Likewise, deciding to enter into a serious relationship with Jesus and his church requires time. Relationships tend to progress gradually as each person reveals himself or herself to the other and feels a growing sense of mutual trust and understanding. We can compare the gradual deepening of a catechumen's relationship with Jesus with the gradual deepening of a relationship between a man and a woman whose love leads to marriage.

Stage of the Process	Love Story
1. Pre-Catechumenate	First dates/encounters
2. Catechumenate	Formal dating
3. Purification and Enlightenment	Engagement and dating
4. Sacraments of Initiation	The wedding ceremony
5. Mystagogy and Beyond	The honeymoon and beyond

1. Pre-Catechumenate: Attention without Intention

I was first introduced to my husband in a formal professional environment, where his lovely eyes and gentle demeanor caught my attention. A couple of weeks later, I ran into him when we were both more casually dressed, and I noticed his hiking boots. Since I really enjoy hiking, my curiosity was piqued, and we began to engage in conversation around this shared passion. We found out that we had a lot in common and began to spend a little more time together.

Every relationship begins with attraction and one person's expression of interest in another. Flirting often takes place to gauge how interested the other is and how serious his or her intention. Sometimes a relationship progresses beyond flirtation; other times it does not. The pre-catechumenate period is the "flirtation" phase of a person's relationship with Jesus and the Catholic Church. This "come and see" (John 1:39) period when people flirt with the notion of following Jesus, Christianity, and the Catholic Church may lead to a relationship, or it may not. During this stage, the "inquirer" flirts with the idea of becoming Catholic based on various factors such as wanting to marry a Catholic, being in a marriage with a Catholic and feeling the stirrings of conversion, or being inspired by some aspect of the Church's teachings that piqued his or her curiosity.

But flirtation is attention without intention. While there may be an attraction to some aspect of the faith, no specific commitment has been made. As the beginning of what will hopefully be a lifelong love relationship with Jesus and his church, this period of the catechumenate is devoted to pre-evangelization and evangelization. There are three things to avoid during this period.

1. Do not try to aggressively "sell" or market Jesus or the Catholic Church. Listen attentively and respond honestly, but resist the urge to overshare at this stage.

2. Do not rush the process. Engage in conversation, but let the inquirer take the lead.

3. Avoid offering detailed catechesis at this stage. If a person is ready for initial proclamation, be sure that the kerygma is presented simply but powerfully.

This inquiry period holds immense opportunities for us. If conducted well, this period of initial attraction leads to an intention to take the relationship further—an intention that is ritualized in the Rite of Acceptance. This is a huge step for many people and marks the inquirer's intention to leave behind the old life as he or she says yes to a new way of living.

2. The Catechumenate: Dating

There comes a time when casual dating becomes more serious. Using our dating analogy, the period during which someone abandons the single life and decides to date seriously is called the catechumenate. This period marks the decision of the catechumen to spend more time learning about and following Jesus and the church. The first ritual step of the catechumenate is the Rite of Acceptance into the Order of Catechumens. In one of the formulas for the Rite of Acceptance, catechumens are asked to "commit your lives daily to his care, so that you may come to believe in him with all your heart. This is the way of faith along which Christ will lead you in love toward eternal life" (*RCIA, Study Guide* 1998, #23, formula A).

This commitment sums up the heart of the process—which ideally is gradual and completed without regard for the constraints of time. Just as in a relationship there is never a set dating period before engagement, neither is there a set length of time for this phase of the catechumenate. Pastoral formation, catechesis, and liturgical catechesis become more comprehensive as the catechumen grows, and include

- learning how to pray and follow the supernatural inspiration of God.
- practicing love of neighbor.
- being formed in the liturgical year, supported by celebrations of the Word.
- comprehensive catechesis, formation in the truths of Catholic doctrine and the moral life.
- sharing in the mission of the Church.

Catechumens are accompanied by a mentor or sponsor during this process. According to the introduction of the RCIA, sponsors are persons "who have known and assisted the candidates and stand as witnesses to the candidates' moral character, faith and intention" (RCIA, #10). The sponsor takes responsibility for mentoring the catechumen but does not have responsibility for formal catechesis. He or she serves as a guide to the Christian way of living so that the catechumen can "catch" the fundamentals of the Christian faith and learn how to apply them in real life using the sponsor as a model. When the catechumen is ready for the celebration of the sacraments of initiation, this period comes to a close with the Rite of Election. Next, the catechumen moves into the period of purification and enlightenment.

3. Purification and Enlightenment: Engagement and Marriage Preparation

After some time, a couple may decide to advance their relationship even further and become engaged. During the proposal, a ring is given, and the couple inherits a new name: they are now known as fiancés. Engagement marks the formal period of preparation for marriage. In the catechumenate process, this period of formal preparation for the sacraments of initiation normally takes place during the Lenten season and culminates with the "I do" of the candidate in the sacraments of baptism, confirmation, and Eucharist at Easter. A commitment is made to a lifelong relationship with Christ and his church. The catechumens are now called the "Elect" and are called to deeper conversion in preparation for renewal at Easter. As in an engagement, when the couple works closely with family and friends to make final preparations for the wedding, the Elect are accompanied by the entire Church on their journey. This is a time of more intense spiritual preparation during which the Elect are instructed gradually, through three "scrutinies," on the nature of sin. The word *scrutiny* comes from the Latin *scrutari*, which means "to search." During the scrutinies, the Elect, along with the entire community, are invited to search their hearts to identify any remaining obstacles to living as a disciple of Christ.

On the wedding day, a couple is asked to profess their vows publicly, and many commit them to memory. During the purification and enlightenment period, the Elect commit the creed and the Our Father to memory and recite them publicly prior to professing faith on the day of their baptism. The purpose of this time is to "purify the minds and hearts of the elect as they search their own consciences and do penance. This period is intended as well, to enlighten the minds and hearts of the elect with a deeper knowledge of Christ the Savior" (*RCIA*, #139).

This purification and enlightenment period is more retreat-like than it is catechetical, with an emphasis on prayer and discernment rather than on study and learning. There should be a marked difference between this period and the catechumenate period. This difference should be reflected in the life of the entire parish community as it slows to a more solemn and prayerful pace and focuses on conversion, baptism, and renewal rather than study and learning.

4. The Sacraments of Initiation: "I Do"

A relationship that began with attraction culminates in marriage. Marriage marks the beginning of two becoming one as the couple unites their bodies, their sufferings, their joys, and their entire lives. When they say "I do" to each other, they say "I don't" to being single or to marrying someone else. Every day the couple will live out the decision to be married in both the ordinary and the extraordinary moments of life.

The celebration of the sacraments of initiation takes place at the Easter Vigil and signifies the new birth of Christians—those entering the Church as well as those who are already Christians. Easter is more than a commemoration of a onetime historic event; it is the rising of Christ here and now in the new lives of those Christians being baptized into the life, Death, and Resurrection of Christ. In saying "I do" to Christ, they say "I don't" to other gods, other lifestyles, and other ways of living. This is the beginning of a new life, and as in marriage, it comes with a new name—the baptismal name. Following baptism and confirmation, the new Christians partake in the Eucharist for the first time.

5. Mystagogy: Beyond the Honeymoon

Following marriage, the honeymoon period is filled with excitement and adjustment as a new way of life is embraced. The couple are now known as newlyweds. During this time, the couple live and make present their marriage vows each day of their lives. The parallel period in the Christian initiation process is called mystagogy, or "study of the mysteries," which occurs after reception into the Church at Easter. The Elect are now known as neophytes. The word *neophyte* can be traced to the Greek *neophytes*: "newly planted" or "newly converted." Like newly married couples who continue to grow in their love and understanding of each other, the neophyte continues to reflect on and learn more about the mysteries of the Mass and the sacraments, in which they now fully participate. There may be bumps along the way, but that is par for the course. Challenges always come when adjusting to a new way of life, but so do much joy and happiness.

As a church, we help our newly formed Christians continue their journey through life's ups and downs. The principal way that we continue to form new Christians is through the celebration of the Eucharist. This period formally concludes with a celebration held on or near Pentecost, but the national statutes for the catechumenate of the United States call for monthly gatherings for new Christians for at least one year after their initiation. Much as one-year anniversaries are celebrated by married couples, anniversary celebrations take place in parishes for new Christians at the end of their first year. And, just as married couples mark their anniversary by reflecting on their wedding day, celebrating all that has happened since and focusing on their future, new Christians are invited to reflect on their journey, give thanks for it, and renew their spiritual commitment to one another during this mystagogical celebration.

The period of mystagogy should continue with strong adult catechesis, which we will explore in detail in the next chapter. There is no graduation for a disciple; the process is one of continued growth in love, learning, and witness of life. Just as there is no formal day on which the honeymoon ends, the period of mystagogy has no formal ending either. Like a married couple striving to pay attention to their marriage for the rest of their lives, those who are baptized are now called to spend the rest of their lives paying attention to their relationship with Jesus.

Religion: A Mystery, Not a Subject

We often speak of religion as a "subject," in much the same way we speak of geography or history. However, it is important to remember that we are not teaching a subject but introducing people to a mystery. This means that our catechesis should incorporate a language of mystery. It should resemble Mass (going to church) more than class (going to school). The catechesis we are called to lead should take its cues from the language of sign and symbol at the heart of the sacramental life of our Catholic faith rather than from the world of education.

Incorporating the language and rituals of worship has the power to transform our catechetical efforts. A simple way to present the kerygma, for example, is to connect it with what is happening at Mass by having a liturgical "prayer focus" in the classroom. This could be a small table covered with cloth matching the liturgical color of the season, along with other sacred objects and items from the natural world and everyday life. Our identity as Catholics springs from the liturgy, and the season in which we find ourselves shapes our spirituality. Nonverbal evangelization is also formative. Every space in which we gather in the presence of God is sacred and is evangelizing. Our goal in catechesis is not simply to provide instruction and transmit information but rather to facilitate transformative encounters with Christ, one person at a time. This is what the RCIA process offers when it is executed well.

Catechesis That Is Informed by the Catechumenate

It is clear that we can no longer have a "business as usual" mentality when it comes to catechesis and parish life. Among the most dangerous words in any organization are these seven: *We have always done it this way.* If we think we can continue to catechize today the same way we have for the last half century, then we are in for a rude awakening. With new generations coming of age and entering adulthood, we are seeing more clearly how our approach to catechesis needs to change.

The catechumenate inspires, energizes, and informs all methods of catechesis. If we look at faith formation through the lens of the RCIA process, it will look radically different from the largely instructional model that is used in most parishes. If we took ample time for relationship building in the pre-catechumenate process, spending time listening to concerns and questions and apprenticing people at their own pace, faith formation could be transformed into discipleship-making communities supporting believers at all levels of faith.

Many of the people who decide to visit a parish are in the minority by choosing to do what their own peers are not doing. They deserve nothing less than our best efforts, time, and resources. We must initiate people gradually into the Christian faith by integrating evangelization, catechesis, and the sacraments. It is time to look at catechesis with fresh eyes and see all the potential it holds for apprenticing and mentoring people of all ages in the faith.

Summary: Good Soil

But as for what was sown on good soil, this is the one who hears the word and understands it, who indeed bears fruit and yields, in one case a hundredfold, in another sixty, and in another thirty. (Matt. 13:23)

The spiritual life cannot be neatly planned. We are called to scatter gospel seeds as best we can and as far as we can. Like gardening, it is time intensive and can get pretty messy! We must remember that the true agent of transformation is the Holy Spirit. We are instruments of God, and while we can do our best to help others grow in faith, the ultimate leap of faith must be taken by those people themselves. Some of our seeds will fall to the ground unnoticed. But others will take root in hearts that are open and ready, to yield a crop that far surpasses what we ever imagined.

For Reflection and Discussion

- What insights regarding the catechumenate are most beneficial to your understanding of catechesis?
- What will you do differently as a result of these new insights?

Growing as a Catechetical Leader

"Changes in the Church's initiation pattern have a powerful effect in the whole life of the Church. How new Christians are initiated affects not only the identity of those initiated but also the self-understanding of the whole church community. That is why RCIA is so vitally important to the renewal of the Church today" (Lawrence E. Mick, *RCIA: Renewing the Church as an Initiating Assembly,* [Liturgical Press, 1989], 31). As cate-

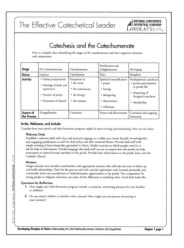

chetical leaders, we benefit immensely from the wisdom of other catechetical leaders—those who have prepared the way for us, those who continue to be a light for us, and those with whom we walk as friends and colleagues. Who has been a spiritual and professional mentor for you? If you haven't seen him or her in some time, call or pay that person a visit. Express gratitude for the mentorship. Similarly, are you aware of struggling catechetical leaders? If so, reach out to them, uplift them in prayer, and offer to help them.

Go to www.loyolapress.com/ECL to access the worksheet.

Suggested Action

"To keep neophytes in mystagogy, you will have to convince them long before Easter that more work follows afterward" (Paul Turner, *The Catechumenate: MI Answers the 101 Most-Asked Questions* [Liturgy Training Publications, 2000], 135). Reflect upon your formation as a catechetical leader. What courses have been most beneficial to you personally and professionally? Make a resolution to strengthen any areas of weakness by taking a class (online or in person) or by reading a book and finding a "study buddy" to discuss them with.

For Further Consideration

The Rite of Christian Initiation of Adults (Chicago: Liturgical Training Publications, 1988).

Beyond the Catechist's Toolbox: Catechesis That Not Only Informs but Also Transforms. Joe Paprocki (Chicago: Loyola Press, 2013).

The Way of Faith: A Field Guide for the RCIA Process. Nick Wagner (New London, CT: Twenty-Third Publications, 2008).

RCIA: Renewing the Church as an Initiating Assembly. Lawrence E. Mick (Collegeville, MN: Liturgical Press, 1989).

"Baptismal Catechumenate: Model for All Catechesis." Catherine Dooley, in *Louvain Studies* 23, no. 2, (Summer 1998): 114–123.

8

Put On Your Own Oxygen Mask First: The Primacy of Adult Catechesis

Shifting Our Focus

When flight attendants provide instructions before a flight, they remind us that in the case of a loss of cabin pressure, adults should secure their own oxygen masks first so that they will be able to assist children in securing theirs. When it comes to faith formation, the same philosophy should apply: Adults should be tended to first so that they, in turn, can assist their children. If we continue to focus our faith-formation efforts exclusively on child-centered catechesis without attending to the needs of our adults, as a church we are going to run out of oxygen and render ourselves unable to help anyone grow in faith.

Adult Catechesis: The Oxygen Mask of Parish Life

I worked with the 157 parishes in the Diocese of Green Bay as a diocesan director of adult faith formation for six wonderful years. Once I was asked at a parish council meeting if I had any dreams for the diocese or for the parishes. I responded by saying that my dream was for adult faith formation to be given the place of prominence that it deserved in diocesan and parish life. "Are you sure about that? We do have a Bible study, you know," the parish council chairperson remarked. "Isn't the dream to have better-attended religious education or youth ministry programs for the children?" another asked.

This conversation crystalizes much of what have been considered the places of adult catechesis and religious education in the parish. When it comes to catechesis of adults and catechesis of youth, it isn't an either-or situation but a both-and one.

Too often, catechesis is thought of as something directed primarily toward children. But the *General Directory for Catechesis* and other key Church documents state clearly that adult catechesis is to be the central form of catechesis toward which all other catechesis is oriented (without detracting from our efforts with children). In *Catechesi Tradendae*, Pope Saint John Paul II remarks that adult catechesis is "the principal form of catechesis, because it is addressed to persons who have the greatest responsibilities and the capacity to live the Christian message in its fully developed form" (#43). Adult catechesis is centered on a lifelong deepening of faith in Christ, thus serving as the point of reference for catechesis in other age groups. Strong catechesis of youth and young adults has its *foundation* in adult catechesis, and we need to plan with this in mind in our parishes.

National Directory for Catechesis reminds us that "because of its importance and because all other forms of catechesis are oriented in some way to it, the catechesis of adults must have high priority at all levels of the Church" (#48a). By securing the oxygen mask of our parish catechetical efforts on adults first, we will be able to ensure that all catechesis at the parish is healthy and vibrant.

Not Your Grandmother's Catechesis

The term *adult religious education* may call to mind seminars, lecture-style formal instruction, or the rehashing of doctrinal formulas learned in childhood from the *Baltimore Catechism*—but none of these images accurately captures the richness of adult catechesis. While adult faith formation includes instruction and the assimilation of knowledge, it also provides many other opportunities for people to grow and mature in faith, such as outreach, service, and spiritual renewal. In her book *Toward an Adult Church* (Loyola Press, 2002), Jane Regan describes adult catechesis as an apprenticeship in the faith, centered around

- information
- formation
- transformation

Information

Information, according to Regan, refers to "all of the ways in which the heart and meaning of the Christian message and the church's tradition are presented in a manner that is meaningful in this time and place" (15). Information invites adults to look beyond the "what" of our faith and instead to answer the question "So what?" In other words, what difference will this learning have upon my attitude, behavior, and practices? Information for information's sake is not enough. We must present information in a way that answers the fundamental questions of life.

Formation

Formation enables adults to move from being passive bystanders to being active, full, and conscious witnesses to their faith. Adults are shaped by forces at the parish, both positive and negative. If a parish does not emphasize the importance of lifelong learning and does not allocate resources or personnel toward the formation of adults, it is likely that adults will perceive adult catechesis as being of little value to themselves and to the community.

Transformation

A systematic process of adult faith formation is one that transforms the lives of believers. The goal of adult faith formation is a personal relationship with Christ, which permeates every area of daily living. Every parish event should be an opportunity for adults to encounter Christ and his living message.

More Than Bible Study

Adult catechesis is filled with challenges, including raising the visibility and awareness of the centrality of this essential ministry. Those involved in adult catechesis know that while this ministry is central to the Church, those in parish leadership too often underestimate the importance of adult faith formation. Adult faith formation may, unfortunately, be viewed as a nonessential ministry in parish life. It is often thought of as a "token" ministry, and if it does happen to be recognized on the parish level, it may be identified exclusively with "Bible study." Adult Catholics in general have been conditioned to think that catechesis is for children and does not pertain to them.

Now, don't get me wrong. I am not saying that there is anything wrong with "Bible studies," only that they should not be the sole focus of adult faith formation at the parish level and the only opportunity for adults to grow in faith. Adult faith formation is far more complex and nuanced than a single approach focusing exclusively on a rotation through various segments of Scripture. There are two foundational considerations that we need to grasp as we look at adult catechesis.

We must abandon the mind-set and the corresponding practice that *programs* disciple people.

Programs are a help, a tool, and a springboard. Having worked in adult faith formation, both at the parish and the diocesan levels, I struggled with the expectation placed on those in adult faith formation that an eight-week DVD program would effectively make disciples. Let me be clear: you cannot pop in a DVD and expect a disciple to pop out the other side of the class. It just doesn't work that way. The disciples walked with Jesus for three years, shared meals with him, were present during his most difficult moments—and yet Peter still denied Jesus three times! Disciple-making is a process, quite often a long one that requires constant patience and abandon to the grace of God.

Adult faith formation happens formally and informally.

Adult faith formation clearly takes place in a variety of contexts and, ideally, outside a classroom setting. It is woven organically into the mission of parish life through social justice, catechesis, outreach, and other forms of ministry. While the church has offered formal instruction for its younger members for centuries, adult formation opportunities have too often been informal and sporadic within the context of normal family and parish activities. While all parish events have the potential to be faith-formative, many adults engage in these events without bringing into focus their own faith or their personal relationship with Christ. We must engage adults both in the parish and in the wider community and help them identify where God is already present in their lives. They will then be able to contextualize their story within the larger story of the people of God.

The Goal of Adult Catechesis: Heartburn

In the document *Our Hearts Were Burning within Us* (USCCB, 1999), the United States Conference of Catholic Bishops sets forth a plan to reinvigorate adult faith formation throughout the United States. This document emphasizes that adult faith formation must be situated at the center of the Church's educational mission rather than relegated to the periphery as it has been for many years. Using the story of the disciples on the road to Emmaus as a guide, the document is an invaluable resource in creating adult programming that is intentional, organized, and systematic in scope and sequence.

Following their encounter with the post-Resurrection Jesus, the disciples exclaimed, "Were not our hearts burning within us while he was talking to us on the road, while he was opening the scriptures to us?" (Luke 24:32). This is the kind of heartburn that we should be aiming for—such a profound change in others that we are all warmed and set aflame by the encounter with Christ.

In *Our Hearts Were Burning within Us*, the bishops outline three major goals of adult faith formation and the necessary steps to guide and direct efforts in adult faith formation (#67–73). They are as follows:

Goal 1. Inviting and enabling ongoing conversion to Jesus in holiness of life

This goal is accomplished by

- helping adults acquire an attitude of conversion to the Lord in order to foster a baptismal spirituality for believers.
- leading adults to recognize and repent of sin, to seek reconciliation through the sacraments, and to cultivate an ever-deepening faith in Jesus.

- putting on the mind of Christ, trusting in the Father's love, obeying God's will, seeking holiness of life, and growing in love for others.
- deepening personal prayer.

Goal 2. Promoting and supporting active membership in the Catholic community

This goal involves

- helping adults to make a conscious and firm decision to live the faith through membership in the Catholic community.
- inviting and supporting baptized adults in their coresponsibility for the Church's mission and life.

Goal 3. Calling and preparing adults to act as disciples in mission to the world

This goal involves

- helping adults become more willing to be Catholic disciples in the world.
- inviting baptized adults to evangelization and a commitment to justice, which is necessary for the transformation of the social and temporal order.

As you plan adult faith formation at your parish, having an understanding of the principles, goals, and objectives of adult catechesis is an important tool in strengthening all catechetical efforts. Whether you are involved in religious education, youth ministry, or pastoral care at your parish, all parish staff are ministers of and to the adults of the parish. Adult faith formation is the purview of all the staff at the parish, regardless of who has the title of adult faith-formation director.

A Glimpse of Jesus

In his book *A Concise Guide to Adult Faith Formation* (Ave Maria Press, 2009), Neil Parent states that "the task of adult catechetical leaders is to help those to whom they minister realize that God is always present to them as teacher—indeed, that God is their primary teacher" (67). Catechesis of adults is essential for the church to carry out the commission given to the Apostles by Christ. In Christ, God reveals to us how we are to live our lives. All adult faith-formation efforts should be Christocentric (with Christ at the center) as we are called to walk side by side with the adults of our parishes, listening to their joys, hopes, sufferings, and doubts. The bishops reflect that "in Jesus the disciples caught a glimpse into the heart of God" (*OHWB*, #11). Those of us who bear responsibility for adult faith formation are also called to bring adults into the heart of God and help them see glimpses of God in all they say and do.

So, what practices should we employ to bring adults into the heart of God? In *Our Hearts Were Burning within Us* (#8–9), the bishops urge us to follow Jesus' example in communicating the Good News. The following five themes emerge:

1. **Accompaniment.** A frequent theme of Pope Francis's pontificate is accompaniment. In *Evangelii Gaudium* (#169), he writes that "the Church will have to initiate everyone—priests, religious and laity—into this 'art of accompaniment' which teaches us to remove our sandals before the sacred ground of the other" (cf. Exod. 3:5). We must first join people in their daily concerns and walk side by side with them on their path of life. Accompaniment is not just for accompaniment's sake, but is always at the service of evangelization and mission.

2. **Presence.** We are called to be present to people, asking them questions and listening attentively as they speak of their joy, hope, grief, and anxiety.

3. **Sharing.** We are called to share the living Word of God with others—a Word that can touch their hearts and minds and unfold the deep meaning of their experience in the light of all that Jesus said and did.

4. **Trust.** We are called to trust the capacity of prayer and sacrament to open the eyes of those we serve to the presence and love of Christ.

5. **Invitation.** We are called to invite others to live and share this Good News in the world.

In his weekly Angelus address on August 19, 2013, Pope Francis remarked that "living the faith is not decorating life with a little religion, as if life were a pie and faith like the whipped cream that you use to decorate it." It is the goal of adult catechesis to create a *lived faith* in adult learners—faith lived in discipleship to Jesus Christ. We cannot be content with forming service attenders who relegate their faith to Sunday morning and drop their children off each week for religious education without taking any steps to grow in their own faith. Faith is not the whipped cream on the pie of life but the very ingredients and the stuff of life. What do the ingredients of a mature faith look like?

Time to Grow Up

In his essay "Followers, Not Admirers," Søren Kierkegaard points out that Christ "never asks for admirers, worshippers, or adherents." Christ always desires us to become his disciples. "It is not adherents of a teaching but followers of a life Christ is looking for. Christ understood that being a 'disciple' was in innermost and deepest harmony with what he said about himself. Christ claimed to *be* the way and the truth and the life (Jn. 14:6)," says Kierkegaard (*Bread and Wine: Readings for Lent and Easter* [Plough, 2003], 55). Immature faith is one centered on admiration; mature faith is the path of discipleship.

A mature faith is one that actively wrestles with the demands of gospel living, has a willingness to live out those demands, and invites others to share in the gospel message. The *General Directory for Catechesis* describes mature faith as "a living, explicit and fruitful confession of faith" (# 82). The goal is to inspire, equip, and shepherd disciples and create disciple-makers who go out to disciple others. Our goal is not to create admirers of Christ who leave their faith at the door of the church. According to the bishops, mature faith, by which a person makes a total and free self-gift to God, has three ingredients.

1. living faith
2. explicit faith
3. fruitful faith

A living faith is

- a searching faith—it seeks understanding.
- conscious and aware of the power and hold of sin in human life.
- longing for the fulfillment of eternal life.

An explicit faith is

- rooted in a personal relationship with Jesus lived in the Catholic community.
- open to a deepening relationship with the Trinity.
- connected to the life, teaching, and mission of the Church.
- confident because it is founded on the Word of God and confirmed by the whole church's supernatural sense of the faith.
- humbly joyful and forms Catholics who are confirmed in what is essential.

A fruitful faith is

- open to the action and power of God's Spirit and enjoys the fruits of the Holy Spirit.

- active and bears the fruits of justice and compassion through outreach to those in need.
- a living witness to the world through the Word but also through the service of love and justice.

A living, explicit, and fruitful faith is nourished by the following practices:

- Frequent reading of the Word of God, the sacred writings of our Tradition, and the official documents of the Church.
- Involvement in the community life and mission of the Church.
- Personal prayer.
- Participation in the works of justice and service to the poor.
- The fulfillment of our human obligations in family and society through the active practice of love for God and neighbor.

Ten Tips for Adult Faith Formation

Our parishes include adults in all stages of the journey of faith. The suggested printable for this chapter includes principles for implementation and planning to help guide your efforts. When planning for adult faith formation, we must consider and design opportunities that will serve the needs and interests of the entire parish faith community and provide

1. quality opportunities for multiple and varied conversion experiences.
2. forums in which to discuss faith learning and faith living.
3. growth in faith through conversations and dialogue with other adults about topics that matter.
4. catechesis to form adults for faithful decision-making.
5. quality activities and events to which parishioners can invite others.

6. promotion and organization of existing activities to shift the paradigm from an exclusively youth-centered catechetical approach to an adult-centered catechesis.

7. diversity in outreach to those of various cultures, particularly the Hispanic population.

8. opportunities to connect with other adults online to discuss the Catholic faith.

9. basic, intermediate, and advanced courses in the Catholic faith.

10. practice and engagement in the spiritual and corporal works of mercy.

Tune Up the Choir!

To move adults toward a deeper commitment to Christ, it is important to empower and equip them with the tools to talk to other adults about their faith. Giving them concrete language and particular strategies to engage people in discussions about the faith will go a long way toward helping adults come to a mature faith. Studies from the Pew Forum and the Center for Applied Research in the Apostolate indicate that the majority of Catholics are in the category of "medium commitment" and will remain so unless actively invited and challenged to move deeper.

Moving our Catholics from medium commitment to active and full commitment in the Church will be a continual challenge for us, but it is sure to pay rich dividends! Often, we overlook those who are sitting right in front of us when it comes to our discipleship efforts. In this case, the cliché "preaching to the choir" does not ring true; we must continually "tune up" the choir through evangelization and catechesis. And the choir includes ourselves. One of the principles of discipleship is that you can lead people only as deeply as you have gone yourself. As catechetical leaders, we must commit to our own growth and continue to pursue a journey of discipleship. The old saying "You can't pour from an empty cup" is true. It's time to fill up the cup so that we can pour for others!

Summary: Called to a Living Faith

Therefore, let us go on toward perfection, leaving behind the basic teaching about Christ, and not laying again the foundation: repentance from dead works and faith toward God. (Heb. 6:1)

In Greek, the word most commonly translated "perfect" is *telios*, which means "brought to its full potential." When we fulfill what we are called to be, we become perfect. Objects become perfect when they do what they are created to do. A plow, for example, finds its fulfillment in the ploughing of the earth. As subjects of the Lord, we find our fulfillment when we grasp our potential and cooperate with God's continual invitation to live in his love and to follow him. We turn away from all the dead things in life that weigh us down, and we turn in faith toward God. This is the call to holiness, the call to sainthood. As catechetical leaders, we are forming disciples for mission who will go out to change the world and help ourselves and others to fulfill their true potential. We might never reach perfection in this life, but we know that, with the grace of God, we are called to journey toward that perfection in thought, word, and deed.

For Reflection and Discussion

- What has been most helpful to me in growing my own faith? Is it a fully mature faith?
- In my ministry, how do I design processes that accompany people from immature faith to mature faith?

Growing as a Catechetical Leader

"Pew researchers found that attending CCD, youth groups, and even Catholic high schools made little or no difference in whether or not an American Catholic teen ended up staying Catholic, becoming Protestant, or leaving to become unaffiliated. The best predictor of adult attendance at religious service is strong adult faith." (*Forming Intentional Disciples*, 34–35). As a catechetical leader, it is easy to

assume that all our catechists are disciples. Our catechists may be at the beginning stage, in the intermediate stage, or at an advanced stage of discipleship. When I consider my catechetical team, how do I make provision for those who are in the different stages of discipleship? What is the one thing I can do to help my catechists grow in faith? Go to www.loyolapress.com/ECL to access the worksheet.

Suggested Action

"Start by listening to adults and let the stories of their lives and the hungers of their hearts inspire pastoral care and inform catechetical programming. Reach out to those whom society often neglects" (*Our Hearts Were Burning within Us*, #80). When I consider the families who have left my faith-formation program, have I stopped to reflect on the real reasons why they might have left? Is there a family whose reasons for leaving you wonder about? In the days ahead, pray about making a personal contact with this family—reaching out to them and listening to why they have left. This takes courage but will be a help to all the families entrusted to your care.

For Further Consideration

Toward an Adult Church: A Vision of Faith Formation. Jane E. Regan (Chicago: Loyola Press, 2002).

A Concise Guide to Adult Faith Formation. Neil A. Parent (Notre Dame, IN: Ave Maria Press, 2010).

Deepening Faith: Adult Faith Formation in the Parish. Janet Schaeffler (Collegeville, MN: Liturgical Press, 2017).

Our Hearts Were Burning within Us (Washington, DC: United States Conference of Catholic Bishops, 2009).

Adult Catechesis in the Christian Community (Liberia Editrice Vaticana, 1990).

9

Go Set the World on Fire: Catechesis through an Evangelizing Lens

Go Set the World on Fire!

Fire has played one of the most significant roles in the advancement of civilization. The world depends on the warmth and energy of the biggest fire near Earth, the sun. Without fire, there would be no life. Fire and life go hand in hand.

This is also true of our spiritual lives. The metaphor of fire is used throughout the Bible to indicate the presence of God, whether directly or through people. God is described as a "consuming fire" (Heb. 12:29); Jesus says, "I came to bring fire to the earth, and how I wish it were already kindled!" (Luke 12:49); and we are told that we will be baptized with the Holy Spirit and fire (Matt. 3:11). Without the fire of our faith, we would be lifeless Christians, lacking fervor and energy. We would have no "get up and go"!

Too often, our approach to faith formation lacks the fire or energy it deserves. Saint Ignatius of Loyola urged his followers to "go set the world on fire!" In this chapter, we will identify opportunities for the catechetical leader to ensure that every aspect of faith formation communicates a sense of passion, energy, inspiration, and mission and helps others burn more brightly.

Fire-Building Essentials: The Rule of Three and Three

Living in Ireland for many years, I became adept at building fires. Many homes have large, open fireplaces around which families gather. One of the first lessons my mother taught me was to always build a fire in layers, placing a couple of pieces of coal on the bottom, adding some light kindling on top, and then stuffing paper in between. Putting on a big log or dumping in too much coal right away would cause a fire to smother and eventually die out. The fire had to be tended regularly so that heat could build up slowly rather than have the fire burn too quickly.

Much as a fire will die out or a circuit will short when it has been overloaded, we as a church have reached what Pope Francis calls a "diagnostic overload" (*Evangelii Gaudium*, #50). This overload, caused by a flurry of activity coupled with dwindling personnel and financial resources, can have the effect of smothering the fire of parish life. If we put more and more activities, events, programs, and stresses on ourselves as ministers, we run the risk of allowing our fires to dwindle down to the bare embers. This danger can be avoided, Pope Francis reminds us, only by an evangelical discernment that prioritizes missionary discipleship. This means a change from a more administrative model of ministry to an evangelical missionary model that emphasizes relationship building. In order to do this, we need to take the kindling of our parish life and plan for a big fire!

Let's start with the fire-building essentials.

During Pope Francis's *Address to the Plenary Assembly of the Pontifical Council for the Promotion of the New Evangelization* (October 14, 2014), he called for "a common commitment to a pastoral plan that recalls the essential and that is well centered on the essential, namely Jesus Christ. It is no use to be scattered in so many secondary or superfluous things, but to be concentrated on the fundamental reality, which is the encounter with Christ, with his mercy, with his love, and to love brothers as He loved us."

A well-thought-out process and vision are necessary for disciple making, and yet many of us in ministry have little experience articulating a long-range pastoral plan. But it is useful to consider a pastoral plan as kindling for the fire. One method for building a healthy pastoral plan is to use what I call "the rule of three and three." This methodology employs three pathways to becoming a disciple-making ministry coupled with three focusing questions, as follows:

1. **Discernment.** Before you undertake any evaluation of the parish or your ministry, view the process in terms of discernment, and permeate the entire process with ample prayer. Objectively assess your ministry, taking time to pray about where the Lord is leading you, while reflecting on the needs of the people you are serving.

2. **Purification.** Identify successes, weaknesses, and opportunities in your ministry. Identify areas for pruning so that new life can occur. Not everything that we do bears fruit, so we must take the time to distill the essential elements of our ministry. Examine what is outdated or no longer working. Take the time to grieve, give thanks for all that was, and look at options for the future.

3. **Reform.** Simplify and streamline your ministry to focus on making disciples of Jesus Christ. Abandon or reform programs and processes that are not in total alignment with this goal.

With these three principles in mind, ask the following questions: In order to form disciples in my personal life and in my ministry, what do I need to . . .

- start doing?
- stop doing?
- keep doing?

Through the years, these questions have been invaluable in helping me distill the essential elements of my ministry. From experience, I can tell you that it is far easier to figure out what we should keep doing and start doing than what we should stop doing. Parishes are unwilling to prune ministries that are no longer bearing fruit and feel more comfortable keeping the existing struggling ministry going while adding new programs or events. As a result, all the ministries struggle because of the constant activity, and so every new ministry is placed in jeopardy before any momentum and fire can be generated.

Many things that we are doing are warming hearts, but we need to look at them in a realistic and healthy way. Jesus tells us to go and make disciples, not bingo players or picnickers. And yet we sometimes spend more time planning for events and setting up tables and chairs than making disciples. Over time this causes our ministerial fire to die down. Every activity should have the goal of leading people to encounter Christ. If you are spending time on activities that do not introduce people to Christ, then stop doing them. While this may sound harsh, it will ultimately free you to put your time and effort into building a fire capable of sustaining itself beyond your wildest dreams.

"Softwood" Opportunities

Getting a fire going is much easier if you use softwood first rather than hardwood. Softwoods are frequently used in building materials and should always be your first choice when building a fire, because they burn easier and faster. In catechetical ministry, building a fire with "softwood" means reaching out to those in the pre-evangelization stage and building trust through creative and engaging opportunities. These opportunities are the "softwood" with which you can build your program more easily, beginning with those closest to you. Hardwood can be added later. Let's explore several "softwood" opportunities that you can incorporate into your catechetical program, beginning with your encounters with parents.

1. Parent Nights: Catechize by Stealth

When I was working in faith formation and youth ministry, many young people shared with me that they never discussed matters of faith with their parents. Those same parents admitted that their faith illiteracy contributed to feelings of insecurity in discussing issues, particularly moral issues, with their children. If my religious education program was to thrive, I knew that I had to strengthen opportunities for parents to connect with their children but also to engage with their peers. I decided to revamp "Parent Night." Instead of discussing matters such as the parish handbook, the cancellation of classes, and so on, I began addressing the Catholic faith in a real, fresh, and simple way. At the time, I often referred to this approach as "CBS"—catechesis by stealth!

Parent nights became a tool for stealthily evangelizing parents who were hungry for community but didn't know how to connect. Usually I titled the program something "catchy" and uplifting. After several parent nights of moderate attendance, parents began stepping forward and asking for more opportunities to learn about their faith. They invited their friends; they requested certain speakers; and they asked for a series of gatherings on topics that interested them.

Through this experience, I learned an important point: we are all ministers *of* and *to* adults. If you work in the area of faith formation, this is an important paradigm shift to make. Youth-centered catechesis cannot happen in a vacuum. We must engage the families and the adults of the community in order to evangelize and catechize our children. Offering parents practical support can help build trust and forge relationships that will make it ultimately possible to share the heart of the gospel message with them.

Here are other ideas to consider from catechetical leaders I've spoken to.

- "Help parents recognize and cope with overscheduling by providing a space where they can discuss real life at the parish. There's no reason that a process of pre-evangelization for parents couldn't be more focused on 'family skills' or parent support founded on gospel principles without dropping the kerygma on them yet."—Jamie W., Colorado

- "Our religious education programs should work in conjunction with adult faith formation to create events and processes that focus on giving parents and families real support in areas that they might need/want. Topics could include budgeting, time management, disciplining children, helping children cultivate good learning habits, communication, etc."—Sandy S., Idaho

- "Implement an adult discipleship course focused on personal conversion in the parish, and draw your catechists from the pool of people who complete it."—Carole B., Oklahoma

2. Disciple Your Catechists: Invest and Equip

At the beginning of this book, we talked about the first audience of the New Evangelization being ourselves. From there we move out to the next closest sphere of influence, which, in our personal lives, is our family. But in the parish, the next closest sphere of influence for catechetical leaders is our catechetical team. Taking the time to invest in our catechists and equipping them with disciple-building skills (proclaiming the kerygma, praying with others, recognizing the signs of discipleship "readiness") means that they can disciple their learners more effectively.

Here are some insights about supporting catechists from ministers around the country:

- "Replicating Jesus in our catechists is critical: helping them encounter Christ, give their lives to him, and then see their work as a catechist through the lens of that relationship. We have seen a marked difference in the fruitfulness of religious education once we required catechists to go through an evangelizing retreat and evangelizing process."—Deacon Keith Strohm, evangelist and author of *Jesus: The Story You Thought You Knew.*

- "Model what discipleship looks like in catechist meetings. Incorporate prayer, lectio divina, and intercessory prayer. Meet with catechists one-on-one. Invest in them as people, build relationships with them so that (a) they want to rise to the level you hope they do because they love working for you, and (b) they are energized to grow themselves because they know they are being invited and being loved into a deeper relationship with Christ. This, of course, also needs to be modeled. Then teach them how to disciple those they are working with and even the parents. Teach them how to build relationships, how to give witness to the faith, how to listen to others, how to ask important guiding and inviting questions."—Jennifer B., Michigan

3. Kerygma: Proclaim and Repeat

The kerygma is essential to the work of making disciples. It is not a onetime event but must be heard "again and again in different ways, the one which we must announce one way or another throughout the process of catechesis, at every level and moment" (Pope Francis, *Evangelii Gaudium*, #164). All formation processes consist of entering more and more deeply into the kerygma.

Here are some suggestions for incorporating the kerygma:

- "The kerygma must be imbedded within every lesson and proclaimed at every opportunity in some way. It has just become obvious to me how nearly pointless it is to talk about anything related to the liturgical year or any other doctrine if we have no grasp of the person of Jesus and the message that he brings."—Rachel E., Chicago

- "In many non-Catholic settings the plan of salvation is repeated. Again. And again. And again. This is critical because not every person is ready to respond at the same age or point. Pope Francis reminds us in *Evangelii Gaudium* that we must never tire of the initial proclamation. Regardless of what curriculum is used or the subject of the lesson, the core of the gospel has to be proclaimed."—Colleen V., Indiana

- "Most parishioners will have two to three interactions with parish staff, so each parish staff member should know how to proclaim the kerygma appropriately to parishioners. For example, confirmation parents should hear the kerygma from our youth minister in some form each week; parishioners should also hear the kerygma in the homily at Mass, and if they read my catechetical articles, they will read a part of the kerygma in them. My goal is for them to be absolutely surrounded by the core gospel message in different ways from different people so that they are inundated with it and it can take root in their hearts."—Jennifer B., Michigan

Adding "Hardwood": Generating Lasting Heat

Once a fire has been lit, it is essential to add hardwood to the fire. Hardwood is slower burning and produces a more sustained and lasting heat. In your faith-formation program, incorporating ideas or models that are more time-intensive and bring about lasting change needs careful discernment and the support of the parish team. These changes can be more difficult to navigate and may have a tendency to "rock the boat," so be sure to consider what layers of change are best to keep the fire burning. Sometimes in ministry we get unpleasant "heat" for various decisions, but adding hardwood is about generating the good kind of heat—lasting change in your faith-formation program for the good of all those whom you serve.

Let's take a look at what other catechetical leaders around the country are doing to generate lasting heat in their programs.

1. Retreat Ministry: Encounters with Christ

One of the challenges in our faith-formation programs is one that remains fixed: time. The challenge of having limited time with students and parents can be an obstacle to relationship building, but it can also help us strive for quality rather than quantity. Plan and design opportunities for children and their parents to encounter Christ, whether it is in weekly prayer or eucharistic adoration or by introducing and reintroducing children and parents to Christ over a longer period.

Here's what two parish communities are doing.

- "One of the best things I've incorporated into my program are grade-level retreats. Every single student attends a retreat every year. I break it into grade groups, K–2, 3–5, 6–8, and high school. These retreats are for the students and their parents. I make sure the parents know that if they don't attend the retreat, their student shouldn't either, since the majority of the retreat is about working together. At the retreats, I give parents tips and tools on how to pass our faith on to the student at that child's level. I always allow time for the parents and students to have one-on-one conversations about varying topics. Every year I have a theme that all the retreats follow, which allows those families with multiple children to learn about the same topic at different levels. I've been doing this for four years and have 80% or higher attendance at each retreat."—Danielle E., Wisconsin

- "Families are introduced to the pathway of intentional discipleship at a weekend family day retreat on the parish grounds. This retreat is offered several times a year and is an entry point for all families with children that desire family formation. The goal is twofold: to allow families to get to know one another and to introduce the pathway of intentional discipleship for families. Our parish centers its vision and mission around three stages in the process of discipleship. Families are called (1) to hear Jesus' call to be his disciple, (2) to give their lives entirely over to Jesus, and (3) to share in Jesus' redemptive mission. In addition to this entry point, another option we offer is for families to meet with one of our staff or lead catechists and share their family story of faith."—Bobby V., California

2. New Models: Building New Fire

Many parishes are taking another look at the traditional classroom model of faith formation and redesigning it or enhancing it. Two examples to consider are as follows:

- "We not only have over-scheduled and stressed families, but limited space at our parish, so we developed a multi-component approach called 'Families Living Faith.' Families attend one 'gathered' day per month in which children are taught in small groups with catechists while parents participate in adult faith formation. Parents teach their children the next two chapters at home with online digital platform assistance. Catechists comment that children are remembering more from year to year, and there's a side benefit—parents are learning as they teach! Included in this approach is a life of the parish component called

'Explore Four,' which focuses on full participation in the life of the parish in one of four areas: prayer, service, learning, and social. Families reflect on and share their experience in the bulletin, on the Web site, on Facebook, in the newsletter, and in the parents' session. This helps our families become evangelizers of other families. We still have parents who do not embrace their role as much as we'd like, but a huge majority of parents do, and the peer pressure to participate is now a very positive pressure. The last two years (and we're in year ten) have been amazing."—Denise U., Illinois

- "We are seeking to build a process where families can have a clear sense of the stages a family goes through in becoming a family of intentional disciples. This would mean that in the near future families would be with other families who are at similar stages of the journey. Families won't merely be grouped and formed together by age, they will be grouped and formed specifically based on where their family is on the journey toward intentional discipleship."—Bobby V., California

Reclaiming the Fire of Parish Life

While our parishes may have weaknesses, they are still the best places to form people in faith for the service of the world. The parish is the people, not just a building or district. The parish is where the people of God come together to become enflamed and go out to share the flame of that faith with others. Evangelization and catechesis must continue to be rooted in the parish. It is the parish that is the first point of contact for most Catholics, particularly those who have been away from the Church and are seeking to return home to the regular practice of their Catholic faith. It is in the parish that we become engaged with the wider Church community, are nourished by Scripture and the sacraments, and have the opportunity for initial and ongoing formation in faith. Parishes must be equipped to see how every aspect of their life and ministry is an opportunity to go out and make disciples of all nations, baptizing the world by the fire of the Holy Spirit.

The true test for us as evangelizing catechetical leaders lies in whether those whom we have evangelized will then go out to evangelize others. As Pope Paul VI remarks, "Here lies the test of truth, the touchstone of evangelization: it is unthinkable that a person should accept the Word and give himself to the kingdom without becoming a person who bears witness to it and proclaims it in his turn" (*Evangelii Nuntiandi*, #24).

The time is now to be pyromaniacs for our faith and set the world on fire!

Summary: That You Bear Much Fruit

"My Father is glorified by this, that you bear much fruit and become my disciples." (John 15:8)

As catechetical leaders, we are asked to bear fruit in our lives and in our ministries. We are asked to bear the fruit of Christian character and Christian conduct in ourselves and in others so that God may have an abundant harvest. Consciously giving and cultivating fruit in our ministries means that we need to be aware of what is flourishing in our ministries and of areas of sparseness and neglect.

As you consider your ministry, are there areas that have gotten out of control and need to be pruned? Are there buds that are growing that need to be left alone to flourish? If we carry out our ministries joyfully attentive to new methods of growing and new expressions of fruit, at harvesttime we will have an abundance. Bearing fruit glorifies God!

For Reflection and Discussion

- Is my fire burning brightly? How does my ministry animate people in the faith? What wood do I need to add to keep it burning?

- What events, activities, or processes might be smothering my ministry?

Growing as a Catechetical Leader

"It is easier to teach a speed-lesson about the Sacrament of Baptism to new parents than it is to sit with them one-on-one to talk about their biggest hopes and greatest fears as new parents. . . . Attend enough classes, complete a program, attend the annual retreat, and you qualify for your First Reconciliation, First Communion and the Sacraments of Confirmation" (Jared Dees, *To Heal, Proclaim, and Teach*, 8). As a cate-

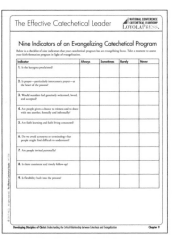

chetical leader, how do I cultivate a program that speaks to people's hopes and diminishes their fears? When I register a new family, for example, do I take the time to sit with them and get to know them and their story so that they feel connected to the parish community?

Go to www.loyolapress.com/ECL to access the worksheet.

Suggested Action

There are many local and national organizations and publications throughout the country that are devoted to catechesis. One such organization is the National Conference for Catechetical Leadership (NCCL), which is the only independent national organization that exclusively serves catechetical leaders. NCCL provides many resources for catechetical leaders, including a monthly magazine titled the *Catechetical Leader*. If you are not yet a member of NCCL, consider joining. If you are a member, whom can you invite to join this organization?

For Further Consideration

A Church on the Move: 52 Ways to Get Mission and Mercy in Motion. Joe Paprocki (Chicago: Loyola Press, 2016).

Rebuilt: Awakening the Faithful, Reaching the Lost, Making Church Matter. Michael White and Tom Corcoran (Notre Dame, IN: Ave Maria Press, 2013).

To Heal, Proclaim, and Teach: The Essential Guide to Ministry in Today's Catholic Church. Jared Dees (Notre Dame, IN: Ave Maria Press, 2016).

Creating the Evangelizing Parish. Frank P. DeSiano, CSP, and Kenneth Boyack, CSP (Mahwah, NJ: Paulist Press, 1993).

10

Your Catechetical Bookshelf:
Church Documents on
Evangelization and Catechesis

Who's Got Your Back?

Typically, when a lawyer is pictured at a press conference, he or she appears in front of bookshelves filled with volumes of lawbooks. The message is clear: this lawyer is backed by the authority of the law and the weight of the legal world.

As catechetical ministers, we, too, are backed by authority—the authority of the Church and the weight of Catholic Tradition. Tradition, when referring to the Church's teaching authority, is often written with a capital *T* to distinguish it from those small-*t* traditions that are customs and practices, not part of divine revelation. The content of Tradition is the true faith itself, given to the Apostles by Christ and faithfully transmitted to each generation.

In our catechetical ministry, we are a part of this Tradition and are guided, supported, and enlightened by numerous pastoral and catechetical documents issued by Church leadership over the years. This chapter serves as an annotated bibliography of Church documents on evangelization and catechesis that every catechetical leader should be familiar with. It also includes a brief description of how Church documents are "weighted."

Authority and the Weight of the Catholic World

With each passing year of college, my backpack seemed to get heavier and my wallet lighter as I bought the necessary books for my classes. When I was a graduate student, my aching back was a reminder that I carried the weight of the Catholic world on my shoulders as I walked to and from class. Our professors told us that these books were an investment in our future—and they were right. When I need to reference something specific on a point of theology, I revisit many of these books. Over the years, I have found myself amassing quite a collection of "must reads" for ministry. Apostolic constitutions, exhortations, and encyclicals nestle side by side on my bookshelf along with declarations and decrees.

With all the documents that have been issued in the past several decades, you might be asking yourself what the differences are among them and how much importance you should attach to them. In general, there are four types of Church documents.

1. Papal documents, which include apostolic encyclicals, exhortations, and constitutions issued by the pope under his own name

2. Council documents, which are issued by ecumenical councils of the Church and promulgated under the pope's name

3. Curial documents, issued by the dicasteries (offices, tribunals, and councils) of the Roman See or the Vatican

4. Bishops' documents, issued by individual bishops or national conferences of bishops

The "weight" of authority behind the various official documents of the Catholic Church depends on the dogmatic history of the teaching and the intention of the Holy Father. Let's look at some of the most common documents and the weight of authority that is attached to them. In order of authority, they are as follows:

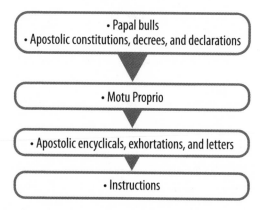

Top Dog: Papal Bulls. Named after the lead seal, or *bulla*, which was once attached to the document in order to authenticate it, papal bulls are reserved for the most formal decrees of the Church—for example, those that clarify doctrine, ratify documents, declare a jubilee, or found a university. Like all papal documents, bulls typically begin with the first words of the official Latin text. When Pope Francis announced the Extraordinary Jubilee Year of Mercy on April 11, 2015, he issued a bull called *Misericordiae Vultus*, which means "The Face of Mercy." The dogma of the Assumption of the Blessed Mother was also issued in the form of a papal bull called *Munificentissimus Deus*, meaning "The Most Bountiful God." Apostolic constitutions, declarations, and decrees are normally issued as papal bulls. Examples of these kinds of documents include the *Catechism of the Catholic Church* and the *Code of Canon Law*. These are considered legislative documents. They contain dogmatic or doctrinal elements and have binding authority on the entire Church.

Pet Projects: Motu Proprio. Legislative matters that do not merit a constitution and are issued by the pope based on his own initiative are referred to as being issued *motu proprio* (from the Latin, meaning "of his own accord"). I like to think of these documents as important pet projects of the pope. They handle specific issues pertinent to the Church during a specific time in history. The document *Intima Ecclesiae Natura* (*The Church's Deepest Nature*), for example, was issued in 2012 by Pope Benedict XVI and clarifies the guidelines for Catholic charitable organizations.

Apostolic Encyclicals. The word *encyclical* means "circular letter." Apostolic encyclicals are papal letters of a pastoral nature that are broad in scope and shed light on doctrine. They are not considered definitive teaching unless they are stated to be such. The salutation of the encyclical captures the audience to which it is addressed. For example, Pope Saint John Paul II's encyclical *The Gospel of Life* (1995) begins with the salutation, "John Paul II to the Bishops, Priests, and Deacons, Men and Women Religious, Lay Faithful, and All People of Good Will on the Value and Inviolability of Human Life." The teaching contained in the encyclical commands respect and assent even though it is not formally declared infallible.

Apostolic Exhortations. These are papal reflections addressed to the Church, the clergy, and the faithful. Ordinarily, they do not contain dogmatic definitions or policies and are not considered legislative. Instead, they exhort or encourage people to implement a particular aspect of the Church's life and teaching. Examples of apostolic exhortations include Pope Paul VI's *Evangelii Nuntiandi* (*On Evangelization Today*), John Paul II's *Christifideles Laici* (*On the Role of the Laity*), Benedict XVI's *Verbum Domini* (*On the Word of God*), and Pope Francis's *Evangelii Gaudium* (*Apostolic Exhortation on the Proclamation of the Gospel in Today's World*). This exhortation followed the Synod of Bishops on the New Evangelization and exhorts the faithful (meaning you and me) to live out the New Evangelization and to proclaim the joy of the gospel throughout the world.

Apostolic Epistles. These letters are usually written in response to a specific need or addressed to a particular group of people. They are usually pastoral in nature and not considered legislative documents.

Instructions. These writings are issued by congregations with the approval of the pope. They amplify the legislative force of apostolic constitutions and outline how they are to be applied. An example of an apostolic instruction is *Liturgiam Authenticam* (*The Authentic Liturgy*), which outlines the implementation of the Second Vatican Council's Constitution on the Liturgy, *Sacrosanctum Concilium*.

Pastoral Letters. These are official documents released by a national conference of bishops such as the United States Conference of Catholic Bishops. They must always be consistent with the teachings of the universal Church and ordinarily require official confirmation by the Holy See to be effective. Examples include *Economic Justice for All: Pastoral Letter on Catholic Social Teaching and the U.S. Economy* and *Marriage: Love and Life in the Divine Plan*, both issued by the United States Conference of Catholic Bishops.

The Essential Evangelization and Catechetical Booklist

Now that we have taken a look at how documents are weighted, let's look at some of the documents and resources that every catechetical leader should be familiar with. When I worked as a parish director of religious education, the *Catechism of the Catholic Church*, the *General Directory for Catechesis*, and the *National Directory for Catechesis* were the "holy trinity" of catechetical books that I consulted frequently in my work. Far more accessible and practical than people realize, the *GDC* and the *NDC* were especially valuable when I was visioning or goal setting in my ministry.

Catechism of the Catholic Church (CCC)

Promulgated as an apostolic constitution by Pope Saint John Paul II in 1992, the *Catechism of the Catholic Church* is a "universal" catechism or compendium of the Church's teaching, designed to be the point of reference for national catechisms throughout the world. It is considered to be a complete and accurate presentation of the Church's teachings and intended to be the principal resource for bishops and catechetical leaders. The *Catechism* is divided into four major parts, which are called the "four pillars." Pope Saint John Paul II called these four pillars the "four movements of a great symphony." They are

1. The Creed (what the Church believes)
2. The Sacraments (what the Church celebrates)
3. The Commandments (what the Church lives)
4. The Our Father (what the Church prays)

The most recent adaptation of the *Catechism* for the context of the United States is the *United States Catholic Catechism for Adults* (*USCCA*).

Compendium of the Catechism of the Catholic Church

Issued by the United States Conference of Catholic Bishops in 2006, the *Compendium of the Catechism of the Catholic Church* offers a clear synopsis of the essential contents of the faith as promulgated in the *Catechism of the Catholic Church*. It is outlined in 598 engaging and accessible questions and answers. The *Compendium* has a four-part structure and includes a section on common prayers and Catholic doctrinal formulas. This is a helpful resource when working with middle- and high-school students, who ask a lot of difficult questions!

General Directory for Catechesis (GDC)

The *General Directory for Catechesis* (1997) outlines the practical and theoretical aspects that link catechesis and evangelization together. Addressed to clergy and catechetical leaders, it should not be considered a how-to manual but a statement of vision, goals, and methods for evangelization and catechesis. The GDC provides religious educators, teachers, and catechists a single point of reference for all aspects of catechetical instruction.

National Directory for Catechesis (NDC)

In the same way that the USCCA is a local adaptation of the *Catechism of the Catholic Church*, the *NDC* is an adaptation of the *GDC* for the Church in the United States. As a companion to the *GDC*, the *NDC* builds on the core themes of the *GDC*, including challenges to catechetical ministry in the United States, opportunities for growth, and ways to link catechesis with evangelization and liturgy. The opening section regarding challenges to the ministry of catechesis is a valuable resource and provides a helpful context for common challenges catechists face in the parish.

Catechesi Tradendae (On Catechesis in Our Time) (CT)

Following the fourth general assembly of the Synod of Bishops held in 1977, *Catechesi Tradendae* (1979) was published. It was Pope Saint John Paul II's first apostolic exhortation on catechesis and religious instruction in the modern world. Particular attention is given to catechesis of young people, so this exhortation should be considered indispensable reading for any catechetical leader.

Evangelii Nuntiandi (On Evangelization in the Modern World) (EN)

An apostolic exhortation of Pope Paul VI, *Evangelii Nuntiandi* is considered to be the "magna carta" on Catholic evangelization and remains relevant and timely. The exhortation affirms the role of every Christian in spreading the Gospel of Jesus Christ and is divided into seven sections, with an introduction. *Evangelii Nuntiandi* defines Catholic evangelization (which is very helpful), the content of evangelization, and the beneficiaries or audiences of evangelization.

Evangelii Gaudium (The Joy of the Gospel) (EG)

Evangelii Gaudium was promulgated by Pope Francis in 2013 after the thirteenth Synod of Bishops in 2012. The theme of the Synod was "The New Evangelization for the Transmission of the Christian Faith." As an apostolic exhortation, the document exhorts, or encourages, all Christians to become missionary disciples so that ecclesial renewal will be lasting and fruitful. The tone of the document is markedly less academic and more informal than previous apostolic exhortations. There are many excellent sections for catechetical leaders regarding lectio divina, prayer, practical tips for evangelization, and the signs of an evangelizing community.

Compendium on the New Evangelization

Published by the Pontifical Council for the Promotion of the New Evangelization in 2015, the *Compendium on the New Evangelization* brings together in one large volume all the foundational documents on the New Evangelization from 1939 through 2012. As a reference book, it is indispensable for tracing the history, expression, and richness of the New Evangelization.

Go and Make Disciples: A National Plan and Strategy for Catholic Evangelization in the United States (GMD)

Published by the USCCB in 1992, this document outlines practical principles, goals, and strategies for evangelization and is intended to provide impetus for action. The document is divided into two sections. The first section outlines the vision and goals for evangelization, while the second section outlines practical strategies for implementation.

Disciples Called to Witness: The New Evangelization

This statement from the USCCB Committee on Evangelization and Catechesis was published in 2013. It focuses on reaching out to Catholics, practicing or not, who have lost a sense of the faith and seek to deepen their relationship with Jesus Christ and his Church. This resource examines the New Evangelization, its focus, its importance for the Church, and how dioceses and parishes can promote it and plan with it in mind.

Our Hearts Were Burning within Us: A Pastoral Plan for Adult Faith Formation in the United States (OHWB)

In this document, which was published in 1999, the USCCB sets forth a plan to reinvigorate adult faith formation throughout the United States. This document continues to be an invaluable resource in creating adult programming that is intentional, organized, and systematic in scope and sequence. The document emphasizes that adult faith formation must be situated at the center of the Church's educational mission rather than relegated to the periphery as it has been for many years. The section on how to form adults in their faith is especially helpful for catechetical leaders as they form their catechists.

Adult Catechesis in the Christian Community (ACCC)

Published in 1990 by the International Council for Catechesis of the Holy See, this document affirms the centrality of adult catechesis and outlines the audience, criteria, and points of reference for adult catechesis. Guidelines for practical implementation are included along with organizational models and methods for implementation.

Guidelines for Doctrinally Sound Catechetical Materials (GDSCM)

Released by the USCCB in 1990, this document outlines guidelines for publishers and other entities to produce catechetical materials that are consistent with the teachings of the Catholic Church.

Sons and Daughters of the Light: A Pastoral Plan for Ministry with Young Adults

In this document, first published by the USCCB in 1997, the bishops offer an effective guide for helping young adults discover the answers to life's most profound questions through a personal relationship with Jesus and the Church.

Doctrinal Elements of a Curriculum Framework for the Development of Catechetical Materials for Young People of High School Age

This document, released by the USCCB in 2008, provides guidance in creating doctrinal content for catechetical texts and materials, curriculum development, and catechetical instruction that define and present the teaching of the Church for those of high school age. This document is a helpful resource for Catholic high schools, parish faith-formation programs, or home-based catechesis.

Adaptation of Doctrinal Elements of a Curriculum Framework for the Development of Catechetical Materials for Young People of High School Age

Released by the USCCB in 2010, this curriculum framework is designed to provide systematic content to guide the catechetical formation of high school students, which takes place in parish religious-education programs and youth ministry programs.

To Teach as Jesus Did

This first pastoral letter of the USCCB was devoted to Catholic education and heavily influenced by the themes and language of the Second Vatican Council. Published in 1972, the document states that "the educational mission of the Church is an integrated ministry embracing three interlocking dimensions: the message revealed by God (didache) which the Church proclaims; fellowship in the life of the Holy Spirit (koinonia); service to the Christian community and the entire human community (diakonia)" (14). An oldie but a goodie!

The Rite of Christian Initiation of Adults (RCIA)

The *Rite of Christian Initiation of Adults* (*RCIA*) was promulgated on January 6, 1972, and the use of RCIA was made mandatory in all U.S. dioceses in 1988. The RCIA is a process through which nonbaptized and baptized men and women enter the Catholic Church, and it includes four distinct stages of formation.

- evangelization or pre-catechumenate
- catechumenate
- sacramental celebration
- mystagogy

Over and Out: The Rest Is Up to You!

With any worthy project, there comes a time when the task ahead
seems so monumental that it can be paralyzing. At one point while
writing this book, I experienced those same feelings and reached out to
a good friend for support and encouragement. He reminded me of the
need for this book among catechetical leaders across the country and
reminded me that twenty years ago, books like this didn't exist. "You
can do it," he reminded me. "You *are* doing it," he said.

Writing a book, I have come to realize, is like childbirth: beautiful,
but very, very painful. Many times I felt like the "little engine that
could" as I chugged and puffed my way through each chapter. *I think I
can, I think I can,* I repeated to myself over and over. Slowly but surely,
the words *I think I can* became *I could!*

Ministry works the same way. It is beautiful but at times also
painful. If you are reading this book and are feeling pangs of anxiety
about the task that lies before you as a catechetical leader, take to heart
the following words from Scripture: "'Everyone who calls on the name
of the Lord will be saved.' But how can they call on him in whom they
have not believed? And how can they believe in him of whom they
have not heard? And how can they hear without someone to preach?
And how can people preach unless they are sent?" (Rom. 10:13–15,
NAB). Your vocation to the ministry of catechetical leadership is no
less than a call from God, who has sent you out to make disciples of all
nations. Your life and ministry constitute an important and necessary
mission in building up the kingdom of God. In his inaugural homily
on April 24, 2005, Pope Benedict XVI reminded us that, like Christ,
we "must set out to lead people out of the desert, towards the place
of life, towards friendship with the Son of God, towards the One who
gives us life, and life in abundance. . . . There is nothing more beautiful than to be surprised by the Gospel, by the encounter with Christ."

We cannot do this work alone, but there is a community of catechetical leaders all across this country—and indeed the world—that will help you and walk with you.

Evangelization and catechesis are the very heart of parish life. The time is now for us to reorient our ministries in ways that speak to the lived experience of people. We have been sent by God to teach, to guide, to evangelize, and, yes, to catechize! Yesterday has come and gone and tomorrow has not yet come. The time is now. It is time to begin.

Summary: Let Down Your Nets for a Catch

When [Jesus] had finished speaking, he said to Simon, "Put out into the deep water and let down the nets for a catch." (Luke 5:4)

As catechetical leaders, we work long hours in ministry. We tend our nets, wait for the catch, and sometimes nothing happens. We do not catch fish. In our tiredness and frustration, sometimes we lose hope.

But in his time, in his own way, the Lord encourages us to set out into the deep and expect an abundance of fish.

Resources were clearly not the problem for the disciples. They had the right resources; they had their nets and boat. But to find fish, they had to go into deep waters. Similarly, we have an abundance of catechetical resources at our fingertips—but we have to go into our own deep waters to find the fish. Many times, we hesitate to put out into the deep because we are afraid to try something new or something different. But Peter teaches us that if we are faithful to Jesus and believe in him with all our heart, great things will happen in our ministries, far beyond what we could ever have imagined. Put out into the deep, catechetical leaders! Are you ready for the catch?

For Reflection and Discussion

- Which Church documents do I consult most frequently in my ministry? Which documents are unfamiliar to me?
- How might I incorporate new learning in my ministry?
- How can I equip my catechists with the most important resources of the Church?

Growing as a Catechetical Leader

For a catechetical leader, familiarity with the guiding documents of catechetical ministry is essential. Sometimes we forget the wisdom of the documents and rely upon certain resources more than others because they are comfortable and familiar to us. Which documents from the above chapter are you unfamiliar with? This year, choose one or two documents to become familiar with, and strive to read and reflect upon these documents throughout the year.

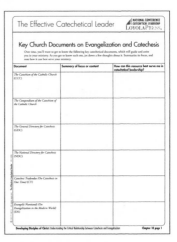

Go to www.loyolapress.com/ECL to access the worksheet.

Suggested Action

Pay attention to the various documents released by the Holy See. Make a resolution to choose one of the documents that you might not have considered reading before, and strive to find a connection between its subject and your catechetical ministry. Make it a point to discuss this resource with one or more of your friends in ministry. Choose a quote or a particular passage from the document that speaks to you, and strive to live out the heart of that sentiment in your ministry.

For Further Consideration

The Catechetical Documents: A Parish Resource. Martin Connell (Chicago: Liturgy Training Publications, 2007).

A Concise Guide to the Documents of Vatican II. Edward P. Hahnenberg (Cincinnati, OH: St. Anthony Messenger Press, 2007).

Scripture and Tradition in the Church. Patrick Madrid (Manchester, NH: Sophia Institute Press, 2014).

About the Author

Julianne Stanz is a nationally known speaker, retreat leader and storyteller who grew up in Ireland. She is the Director of New Evangelization for the Diocese of Green Bay and a consultant to the USCCB Committee on Catechesis and Evangelization. Julianne is married with three children and spends her time reading, writing, teaching and collecting beach glass.

The Effective Catechetical Leader Series

Whether you are starting out as a catechetical leader or have been serving as one for many years, **The Effective Catechetical Leader** series will help you use every aspect of this ministry to proclaim the Gospel and invite people to discipleship.

Called by Name
Preparing Yourself for the Vocation of Catechetical Leader

Catechetical Leadership
What It Should Look Like, How It Should Work, and Whom It Should Serve

Developing Disciples of Christ
Understanding the Critical Relationship between Catechesis and Evangelization

Cultivating Your Catechists
How to Recruit, Encourage, and Retain Successful Catechists

Excellence in Ministry
Best Practices for Successful Catechetical Leadership

All God's People
Effective Catechesis in a Diverse Church

Each book in **The Effective Catechetical Leader** series is available for $13.95, or the entire series is available for $65.00.

To Order:
Call **800.621.1008** or visit **loyolapress.com/ECL**

The ECL App

Everything You Need to Be an Effective Catechetical Leader

The ECL app puts wisdom and practical help at your fingertips. Drawn directly from the six books of **The Effective Catechetical Leader** series, ECL provides an opportunity for catechetical leaders to center themselves spiritually each day, focus on specific pastoral issues, and identify go-to strategies for meeting the challenges of serving as an effective catechetical leader.

Special Features:

- Over 40 unique guided reflections tailored to your individual pastoral ministry needs.
- On-the-go convenience and accessibility on your phone or tablet.
- Modern design, easy-to-use interface, and a source of calm amidst the busy schedule of a catechetical leader.

For more details and to download the app, visit **www.loyolapress.com/ECL**